AF505432

PEACE IN THE MAKING

Proceedings of the Third Asia-Pacific Roundtable
Kuala Lumpur, June 16-19, 1989

Edited by Rohana Mahmood

Published by
Institute of Strategic and International Studies (ISIS) Malaysia

Distributed by
Kegan Paul International

London and New York

© ISIS Malaysia 1990

First published in 1990 by ISIS Malaysia
PO Box 12424
50778 Kuala Lumpur, Malaysia
Tel 03-2939366
Telex MA31679
Fax 603-2939430

Distributed by Kegan Paul International Ltd
PO Box 256
London WC1B 3SW, England
Tel 071-580-5511
Telex 261771 KEGANP G
Fax 071-436-0899

International Edition

ISBN 0 7103 0419 6 (hard cover)

ISBN 0 7103 0420 X (soft cover)

Printed by Art Printing Works Sdn Bhd

British Library Cataloguing in Publication Data
Asia-Pacific Roundtable : 3rd : 1989 : Kuala Lumpur,
    Selangor
    Peace in the making : proceedings of the third Asia-Pacific Roundtable
    1. Pacific region. International Security
    I. Title II. Mahmood, Rohana
    327. 116,
    ISBN 0-7103-0419-6
US Library of Congress Cataloguing in Publication Data
Applied for

Contents

Preface

1989 was an epoch-making year. It was the year the post-war world — in form, if not in substance — capitulated. If there was anything the main events of 1989 were hinged to, it was the momentum of change that began much earlier — when the superpowers, the Soviet Union in particular, began in earnest to place economics before ideology, confidence before conflict, and truth before dogma.

The Tiananmen incident, the Gorbachev-Deng summit, the Soviet and Vietnamese withdrawals from Afghanistan and Cambodia respectively, various attempts to solve the 11-year Cambodia conflict, and to cap it all, the collapse of communism in Eastern Europe are part of this continuum of interlocking events.

Participants to the Third Asia-Pacific Roundtable, held in Kuala Lumpur from July 16-19, 1989, could not have foreseen the breadth and speed of many changes that took place towards the end of the year. They did, however, manage to discuss how peace in the Pacific was in the making in tandem with the mood for change felt globally.

Sino-Soviet relations reached a 30-year high and the ties between the Soviets and the Americans had never been better since the end of World War II. There were signs of thaw in Soviet-Japanese and Asean-Indochinese relations and between the two Koreas. Many people were hopeful then that the Cambodian conflict would come to an end before the year was over.

The Roundtable, the only forum in the world to discuss political and security issues of concern to the region, was attended by 121 participants from all over the Pacific — Brunei, Indonesia, Malaysia, the Philippines, Singapore,

Thailand, the United States, the Soviet Union, Australia, Britain, Myanmar, Cambodia, Canada, China, Fiji, France, Japan, South Korea, North Korea, Laos, New Zealand and Vietnam.

The discussion dealt with:

- The Soviet-American dimension;
- The Sino-Soviet dimension;
- Soviet-Japanese relations in the short, medium and long term;
- Sino-Vietnamese relations in the short, medium and long term;
- The Korean conflict in the short, medium and long term; and
- Political Settlement of the conflict in Cambodia.

Two workshops were held to record areas of agreement with regard to confidence building and conflict reduction *vis-a-vis* the Korean and the Cambodian conflicts.

This volume comprises eight papers and the keynote address presented together with the reports of the two workshops. It is the hope of ISIS Malaysia that this volume, together with the two previous publications — *In Search of Peace* and *Building Confidence, Resolving Conflicts* — will be of value to researchers and policy-makers interested in peace and stability in the Asia-Pacific region.

We would like to express our appreciation to the writers for kindly allowing ISIS Malaysia to publish their papers. Our gratitude also goes to the Canadian International Development Agency (CIDA) and to all who have contributed to this publication.

ROHANA MAHMOOD
Analyst, ISIS Malaysia

Beyond confrontation: The challenge of peace in the Pacific

DATO' SERI
DR MAHATHIR
MOHAMAD
*Prime Minister,
Malaysia*

PLEASE allow me to say what a pleasure it is for me to bid a warm welcome to such a large and august gathering, meeting in this small capital of a small nation in the Western Pacific. The fact that we have in this very room important men and women of thought and action from every band of the political spectrum bears testimony to the momentum of peace in the world and the Pacific today.

This momentum of peace cannot be taken for granted. Many of the most promising trends of recent years can be turned around. Many things can still go wrong — through errors of omission, mistakes in calculation, failures in domestic and international statesmanship. We ought always to be reminded that in international relations there are no brave and benign new worlds and no miracles. We would be foolish to presume that beyond the age of confrontation which we have all endured. for so long lies, necessarily, a new era of cooperation.

At the same time, there can be no denying that not for two generations has there been such a positive constellation of positive political factors in the global firmament. I put it to you that we have entered into an era of great transition, affording immense opportunity, demanding of enlightened action and creative initiative. If we are up to the imperatives of statesmanship, the dictates of enlightened action and the challenges of creative initiative, there is every probability that the last decade of the 20th century will — in political terms at least — be a much better one than what we have seen in the last 50 years. Again, we must guard against excessive optimism. But the auguries are good. Allow me to briefly outline some of the very positive and fundamental changes that have occurred, sometimes at speeds that test our very ability to clearly comprehend their content and their implications.

When historians write about the 20th century, they will need to grapple with an explanation of the role that ideology played globally in the relations between so many nations over some eight decades, a conflict over ideas and systems.

There has of course never been a time when ideology has counted for nothing. There will never come a time when it counts for nothing. In the apparent death throes of the 20th century's heroic Age of Ideology, we can expect some ideological contention between the various believers of capitalism and between the various believers of the command economy. We might even expect on occasion sharp ideological altercation between the leaders and would-be leaders of what has been the Great Ideological Divide. But it does seem a safe conclusion that because of the fundamental reassessment of socialism as a method worldwide and because of a host of other factors, we can at last expect the passing of the Age of Ideology as we have known it. More and more, we can expect ideology to be less and less important in international relations — as pragmatism and the traditional imperatives of national interest come increasingly to the fore.

The second, related, positive factor is the process of internal reform and restructuring amongst the great and the big powers, the most consequential being the turning inwards of the great anti status quo powers.

China was the first to institute a comprehensive programme, which it called the Four Modernisations. The recent tragic events in China, not unconnected with the problems of economic success, are likely to tie the Chinese leadership down to internal preoccupations.

The Soviet Union, under the ambitious leadership of Mikhail Gorbachev, is now already knee-deep in an equally comprehensive and very difficult programme of *glasnost* and *perestroika*. Japan too is in the process of fundamental — economic and societal — change. The European Community can be expected to be greatly diverted by the process of single-market completion by 1992. There are many who expect the United States itself — under the cautious leadership of George Bush — to embark on internal reassessment intended to re-establish its vitality and strength, and to re-establish what some have called the *Pax Americana*.

The two superpowers which have sacrificed substantially because of their strategic overstretch are in the process of strategic disengagement. Because the costs to the United States have been of a different order, its reconsideration of commitments and international activism will be of a different order. Because the Soviet Union has been the nation which has paid so dearly for its strategic overstretch, we have already seen dramatic examples of disengagement and retrenchment. Great changes are in train in Eastern Europe and in other parts of the globe. The transformation taking place in the Second World is nigh irreversible. We should be equally clear in our minds that the positive moves of the

Soviet Union are largely the result of internal imperatives arising out of the nation-centric desire to improve the welfare of the Soviet peoples. This does not detract, however, from their positive impact on the global scene. Indeed, it provides a more secure foundation than would such motivations as an unsustainable starry-eyed commitment to peace or ideology.

Because of all these factors, there are those who believe that the cold war between the Political East and the Political West has now come to an end. I prefer to cautiously believe that the rumours of the death of the titanic contest of systems which has been one of the central hallmarks of the 20th century are somewhat premature. It is still too early to write the epitaph on the cold war.

But who can deny that there is today a historic opportunity to once and for all put to an end a conflict which has engaged so many and so much of the passions of this century? Surely no one can deny that many regional conflicts are being actively addressed and we have entered a period of increasing *detente*. At the global level, there has been a fundamental reduction of tensions between the United States and the Soviet Union.

In the Pacific, the cold war between Moscow and Beijing is largely at an end. Although the consequences of the events in China cannot now be fully fathomed in terms of international relations, we have in recent months and years seen some easing of tensions between Beijing and Taipei, between Beijing and Seoul, between Beijing and Hanoi, between Bangkok and Hanoi, between Thailand and the other countries of Indochina, and between these countries and Asean.

All this is tied to two other important realities: the realisation of the limited power that can come out of the barrel of the gun and of the virtues of extension by other means. In the course of time and since the dawn of the nuclear age, the very essence of power has been substantially transformed. What is more, this is increasingly being perceived by governments and peoples.

There was a time when one scurvy-infested gunboat might have been enough to topple regimes. Let us not forget the consequences of four black ships upon Japan. A thin red line, backed by a thin line of naval power, did play an unbelievable role in the creation of an empire on which the sun never set.

Yet in the world of today, the might of the Americans was not enough in the case of Vietnam. The might of the Soviet Union was not enough in the case of Afghanistan. As many of us have seen with our own eyes, one solitary man can halt a column of heavy tanks. The two superpowers are at the peak of their military might, with almost godlike ability to obliterate every living thing on this planet many times over, even as their political power has been on the wane — in a world that has increasingly become multipolar and promises to be much more so.

Although the writing has been on the wall for decades, it is today writ in such large and bold letters that even the near illiterate and the myopic can now read the message.

The path to disarmament, armed preparedness and deterrence at lower levels of lethality and higher levels of sanity will by no means be easy. The military-industrial complexes can be assured that never will swords be turned into ploughshares. But we can now expect most nations to subscribe to the concept of reasonable sufficiency. More and more governments are likely to come to the conclusion that enough is enough.

Given:

- the increasingly prohibitive financial, political and other costs of war,
- the increasingly limited circumstances under which it will appear rational,
- the increasing difficulty generally of converting military capability into political power,
- the increasing preoccupation of the big and super powers in domestic development and their increasing awareness of the comprehensive costs of military overstretch,
- the dramatic attenuation of the cold war,
- the lessening of tensions at the global, regional and local plane, and
- the decrease in ideological fervour and passion,

we can reasonably expect fewer international wars and fewer international wars of size. There are two other reasons why there are grounds for being optimistic with regard to the surging tide of peace that is characteristic not only of the Pacific but also of other parts of the world.

The first is the demonstrable efficacy and virtues of war by other means and national extension by other methods. The second is the fact that we have entered an era most likely to be characterised by the primacy of economics.

The world has learnt many lessons from the Japanese with regard to business and management. Japan has also been an exemplary state with regard to one important strategic lesson: that the objectives of a state can be achieved through the use of economic means — to the great welfare and benefit of the subject state and, in most cases, to the benefit and welfare of the object state.

A case can be made that we have already moved into a period of 'soft imperialism' where the foundations of a nation's power are more likely to rest on brains rather than brawn, on the creativity, energy and talent of its people rather than on the size of its population and the extent of its territory.

Increasingly, it can be argued, national prosperity and political power will hinge not on the lands that an army can conquer and the number of people that a nation can subjugate but on the degree of penetration of markets, the extent to which other peoples are reliant on one's financial flows, technology and domestic market, the extent to which they are dependent on the products that one can provide and the services that one can render. Much of the virtue of this soft imperialism lies in the fact that the so-called target may aid and abet and certainly welcome one's national extension.

Again, there is need for caution because what is soft can become hard. Soft imperialism too can be perverted by the desire for pomp and glory, and by the will to dominate and to dictate. But conducted in an enlightened and therefore sustainable manner, this soft imperialism is not a zero-sum game. Indeed, it is a process that promises a wealth of mutual benefit — because the interest of the expansionist power is inherently and critically tied to the comprehensive prosperity of the countries which are its targets.

If I am right and what we will see in the years ahead are increasing examples of economic expansionism and decreasing attempts at military expansionism, then we can expect much more of our future to be determined by the trading state rather than by the garrison and the military state.

This will contribute to the rise of the primacy of economics, a trend that cannot but come increasingly to the fore as ideological passions are dissipated, as the cold war winds down, as resort to military means is reduced, as the big powers, the superpowers and the small powers turn increasingly to economic development and social welfare. There are two other very important reasons why economics will play an increasing role in the affairs of nations.

First, the world is likely to be forced to grapple more and more with a host of intractable international economic issues. The statistics testify to the fact that since the 1960s the trendlines for global economic growth and international trade growth have been on a clearly downward path. In the year ahead and in the years to come most nations will have to deal with the most serious economic issues because of the mammoth structural imbalances of the US economy, the primary engine of global growth since the early 1950s, which must be expected to lose steam. The problem of increasing protectionism, trade blocs, currency volatility, international debt, the malaise of the large majority of developing countries, will all take the time of our diplomacy and test the calibre of our domestic and international economic management.

The second reason is also altogether too clear: the rise of economic conflict. Many of the root causes of the present economic friction and of the future escalation of economic contradictions are plain. It is important here to note a central paradox of economic conflict at this point in world history.

Whereas in the case of ideological, political and military conflict the struggle is most often and most intensive as between states that are not interdependent and that are not close, it is in the inherent nature of economic conflicts that they will be most numerous and most intense as between states that are closely interdependent and deeply interpenetrated. Whereas ideological, political and military conflict has been essentially between adversaries and enemies, economic conflict is most likely as between friends and allies. Whereas in the era of ideological, political and military confrontation what is crucial is the containment of adversaries and enemies, in an era of economic conflict the central task is likely to be the management of friends and allies.

What will be the outcome of escalated economic contradiction in a world where the traditional and great Communism-Capitalism, East-West conflicts are no longer the central frame of reference? How will the new lines of friction and contention be drawn when the old lines of division are blurred or are no longer fully operative?

I have warned against excessive optimism and the need, as always, for complete realism. I think I have hinted that there are dangerous elements in the evolving strategic picture which should be cause for serious concern. None of this detracts from the reality that this is indeed a time of opportunity. And history will not forgive us if, through errors of omission, weakness of purpose, perversity of vision, we allow the opportunities for peace to slip through our fingers. Allow me to reiterate: the need of the hour is for enlightened action and creative initiative.

But what must be the elements of such enlightened action and creative initiative? As the Prime Minister of a small country, I feel it necessary to stress that one of the misconceptions that must be jettisoned at the start is to believe that the smaller states have no role or no significant role to play. To be sure, in the great affairs of men, few can make a difference. But all must try. If it can be said that acquaintanceship with power tends to corrupt, it can also be said that a sense of powerlessness also tends to corrupt. The first is the corruption of power. The second is the corruption of powerlessness.

I believe that there is no nation that is too small to contribute to peace in the Pacific. In this regard I am reminded of the ancient Arabian saying that if each man sweeps before his door, the whole street will be clean. At the very least, each nation can contribute to peace if it puts its own house in order, if it develops its national resilience and if it seeks the dignity and chooses the high ground of independence. We can do much more — without waiting for a nudge from the big powers, at the behest of our own persuasion.

In Southeast Asia itself, a part of the world that has been characterised for much too long as a region in turmoil, we have seen how a group of five states went about to create a secure zone of peace and freedom for themselves. Since memories are short, perhaps I should remind you that in the mid-1960s what is now the Asean Community consisted of states many of which did not even know each other, disliked each other or were in a state of confrontation, cold confrontation or even hot military conflict. In a creative act of regional reconciliation, the Asean Five decided to create a different world for themselves.

What exists today is a community, now expanded to six nations, where there is securely in place a structure of understanding and trust, goodwill and active cooperation unprecedented in the history of Southeast Asia. There were many obstacles in the way and more than just hiccups. But what we have now firmly established is a *Pax Aseana*, the more remarkable because it is a Peace without an imperium. It might also be noted that the Asean Community constitutes three-quarters of Southeast Asian real estate. It is where three out of four Southeast Asians live and where more than nine-tenths of Southeast Asian income is generated.

Among the things we have done is to firmly establish an effective code of inter-state conduct based on the principles of peaceful co-existence. Central to that effective code are mutual respect for the sanctity of borders and absolute intolerance of military aggression. Asean's horizon from the very beginning was Southeast Asia as a whole. Its purpose from the very beginning was to turn a region in turmoil into a region of peace and cooperative co-existence. It was for this reason that we could not tolerate and had to oppose the Vietnamese invasion of Cambodia.

Today, we must continue to be patient and to ensure the total removal of Vietnamese troops from Cambodia. There is now every confidence that this will be done by the end of September. It is important that Hanoi's word be kept. The traffic cannot move until the obstacle is out of the way.

Even as we wait patiently, it is essential for the Asean states to now hammer out the acceptable modalities and the most appropriate institutions. We must stand ready to launch the second phase of regional reconciliation, to achieve our ultimate objective: the creation of a Southeast Asian system of states that are at peace with each other, involved in a dynamic and vigorous relationship of mutual respect and mutually beneficial cooperation.

We must not be at sixes and threes. The mountain of distrust and misunderstanding must be removed. A divided Southeast Asia is not in the interest of any regional state. It is in the interest of all of Southeast Asia that we secure a healthy balance of forces, a system open to the world, composed of states which are economically prosperous, socially dynamic, strategically secure, domestically at peace and politically at one.

To ensure all this and to prevent hegemonism from any quarter, we of Asean must be prepared for a comprehensive and creative engagement of all the large powers. And we must be prepared for the comprehensive and creative engagement of Burma, Vietnam, Laos and Cambodia.

I strongly urge all the external powers — from the north, south, east and west, from the first, second and third worlds, from the mature states of western Europe and the new, dynamic states of northeast Asia — to come to Southeast Asia to play legitimate and constructive roles that will be to the benefit of all. I also support fully the objective of transforming Indochina from a battlefield into a marketplace, a process in which we in Asean can play an active role, but a transformation nevertheless that has to be accomplished by the states of Indochina themselves.

I have stated that so much depends on the removal of Vietnamese troops. That the Vietnamese must do. But Asean must be prepared to play a fully constructive role in the removal of that roadblock and to ensure the emergence of a Cambodia that is independent, neutral, non-aligned and, very importantly, peaceful.

It would be a tragedy if there is a return to genocidal policies. The Cambodian people have suffered enough. We must all do our utmost to prevent the outbreak of civil war.

The comprehensive political settlement that we must work determinedly towards must be one that is moral, that is viable and that is productive. Such a solution must recognise the realities on the ground, in the region, and of international politics. Such a solution must secure a meaningful place for Prince Norodom Sihanouk.

As the Prime Minister of a small state, I have necessarily stressed the role that small states can play with regard to the process of peace in the Asia-Pacific region. As a realist, I must emphasise the great role that the great powers have to play in the process of reducing tensions, building confidence and resolving conflicts. Important though they are, the contribution that the great powers make must extend beyond the creation of better atmospherics.

The United States and many other states have poured a great deal of cold water on the Soviet Government Statement on the Asia-Pacific Region of April 1986, Mr Gorbachev's Vladivostok speech of July 1986, his speech to the Indian Parliament of November 1986, his *Merdeka* interview of July 1987, his Krasnoyarsk speech of September 1988 and his United Nations speech of December 1988. To be fair, there are elements in each of these initiatives which are cynically self-serving of Soviet interests, worthy of a place in the recesses of the Cold War. The Krasnoyarsk speech was made at a critical juncture in the US-Philippines negotiations over Clark and Subic. How are we to treat the proposal that Hiroshima be the Helsinki of the Pacific? Many of the proposals thus far put forward are deserving of a great deal of cold water and hot indignation.

It is important that good, negotiable proposals are not contaminated by the company of suggestions that are clearly mischievous, or that will be seen to be mischievous and thoroughly cynical. It is essential that the initiator is fully sensitive to the interests, perspectives and sensitivities of the other party. It is important that neither party is thrown on the defensive. It is crucial that no initiative is seen to be intended specifically for that purpose.

At the same time, many of the moves of the Soviet Union should not be rejected in toto and are worthy of the most serious consideration. Mr Gorbachev's suggestion of prior notification with regard to big naval exercises and for 'the joint elaboration of measures to prevent incidents in the open sea and the airspace above it', for example, deserve serious study. And there truly are possibilities for measures to enhance confidence and to guard against accidental military clashes arising out of miscalculation, misperception and technical mistakes such as we have seen in the Persian Gulf.

Apart from prior notification of major military manoeuvres, there are possible measures to increase 'transparency' through information exchange. A hot-line between the headquarters of the two superpower military establishments in the Pacific and regular dialogues between their military personnel could be of some use; the first in the context of crisis situations, the second in order to reduce the present level of ignorance and prejudice on all sides.

Let me conclude by reiterating that we are poised at a point where we can go beyond confrontation to something better. But we cannot move from here to there if minds are closed, if we are unwilling to think new thoughts, and if we take into a transformed world that will be the 1990s all the heavy intellectual baggage of the age of confrontation.

It has been said that advice is something that the wise do not need and that fools will not take. Assuredly, those who will not be counselled cannot be helped. I hope that I have not sounded the incurable optimist. I believe that meetings such as this Third Asia-Pacific Roundtable can play a most constructive role in generating new ideas, in reducing prejudices, in subverting ignorance, in creating new atmospherics — and in coming forth with advice on how we can all move forward. I have every confidence that individually or as a group you can play a meaningful role. We must move effectively forward with regard to confidence building and conflict reduction in the Pacific and the wider world. Upon this will hinge the judgement of history and our hopes for building a better future.

Sino-Soviet normalisation and Asia-Pacific security

GAO E
Deputy Director-General, Centre for International Studies, China

THE historic May 1989 Sino-Soviet summit marks the eventual normalisation after a 30-year estrangement, ends the past, opens up the future, and highlights a new point in Sino-Soviet relations. This outstanding event in current international politics will certainly have a big impact on Asia-Pacific stability and the global situation as a whole.

A tortuous path characterises the past four decades of Sino-Soviet relations. The rapprochement — on a new basis with an epoch-making significance — has been hard won, recording substantive progress in eliminating obstacles to normalisation through common endeavours in recent years. To be sure, normalisation will boost Sino-Soviet ties in politics, economics, trade, technology, culture and other fields. This fits in well with the fundamental interests and urgent aspirations of the people of the two countries. However, to sustain a healthy, steady development of this process, satisfactory solutions to existing problems have to be found through greater, mutual efforts in the future. A single summit meeting could not sweep away all the problems accumulated in the past or iron out differences of opinion on some issues. Nevertheless, the summit has set a good example in carving out a brighter future through a retrospective summing-up of the past, thus offering some beneficial experience in tackling other complicated international issues in future.

The annals of the chequered history of Sino-Soviet relations can be sketched out in the following phases: Harmonious alliance spanning from the establishment of diplomatic ties up to the end of the 1950s; strain and hostility in the

1960s and 1970s; transition to gradual relaxation of tensions since the advent of the 1980s; and finally, a new chapter of peaceful co-existence brought about by the 1989 normalisation. Such a tortuous process has taught both sides sufficiently rich lessons to enable them to reach an agreement to set up a new type of relationship on a fresh political cornerstone. However, the mutually confirmed principles governing future Sino-Soviet relations have nothing in common with those of the days of intimate alliance nor with those of the years of hostility and confrontation.

A tidal wave transforming confrontation into dialogue and tension into relaxation is surging through the world today, mirroring profound changes in the international situation. The post-World War II picture of US-Soviet dominated East-West confrontation has been blurred, and a new multipolar world is in the offing. Increasingly, the rise and fall of a country and its status in the international community will be conditioned by its comprehensive national strength, especially its place on the global economic and scientific-technological ladder. Awakening to the fact that superpower position can no longer be sustained by military muscle alone, both Washington and Moscow are bent on making readjustments in their respective development strategies. Indeed, peace and development have turned out to be two major themes facing the contemporary world. Flowing with the stream of history, Sino-Soviet normalisation has enriched this process.

Next, removal of ideological/theoretical trammels has resulted in a changed international situation, thus necessitating a more realistic analysis of the current world, a new understanding of the developments of modern capitalism, and deep reflections on socialism coupled with a casting aside of the obsolete 'one model only' idea. Such ideological/theoretical progress has broadened the scope for setting up a new type of relationship between China and the Soviet Union.

Finally, ongoing political/economic restructuring in the two countries in their search for new approaches to socio-economic development under socialism has aroused interest in mutual understanding and stimulated hope for the two to exchange information and draw lessons from one another in tackling problems encountered in the course of reform and development. The deepening and unfolding of reform on both sides have thus given an impetus to the normalisation process and opened up new fields for cooperation and exchange.

China and the Soviet Union are not only neighbours but also major powers with one-quarter of the global population and a common border of over 7,000 kilometres. Just as construction and development in the two countries have a bearing on the progress of mankind, so does their improved relationship exert a considerable impact on the changes in the international situation. It is quite natural that the direction of this improved relationship has attracted the attention not only of the Chinese and Soviet people but also of the people in other parts of the world.

However, the Sino-Soviet normalisation has caused some anxiety about a possible return to the 'comradely', 'alliance-type' partnership witnessed in the

1950s. The Sino-Soviet joint communique has made it clear that a new type of relationship will be forged between the two countries on the basis of the universal principles guiding state-to-state relations, namely, mutual respect for sovereignty and territorial integrity, non-aggression, non-interference in one another's internal affairs, equality and mutual benefit, and peaceful coexistence.

In fact, both sides are aware that steady and healthy development of future bilateral relations will be possible only through faithful observance of the Five Principles of Peaceful Coexistence. Furthermore, post-World War II practice of international relations has proved that these Five Principles are applicable to relations not only between countries with different social systems, but also between countries with similar social systems. The explicit designation of the Five Principles as the basis for future Sino-Soviet relations represents a major step forward in enlarging their scope of application.

Normalisation of inter-party relations automatically follows normalisation of state relations. The two sides agreed that inter-party relations should be built on the basis of four principles of independence, complete equality, mutual respect and non-interference in one another's internal affairs. This sensible approach has thus precluded many factors of disturbance seen in the past.

In essence, the Sino-Soviet alliance was the outcome of the 1950s cold war. Under the then strained international relations, acute confrontation existed between the two camps of capitalism and socialism, and dominated by military confrontation in the form of military alliances, blocs or bases. The direction of international affairs was then the monopoly of Washington and Moscow, propped up by their respective positions of strength. Created in such a severe international situation, yet to be recognised by a large number of countries, notably Western countries, and faced with a hard reality of military strangulation and economic blockade, the New China could only opt for a foreign policy of 'leaning to the side of socialism' and sign the Sino-Soviet treaty of friendship, alliance and mutual assistance with its northern neighbour, without any other alternative in sight. The correctness of this approach has been vindicated by realities. Back in the 1950s, Sino-Soviet solidarity and cooperation had not only defended New China's independence, guaranteed its economic recovery and progress, and frustrated the imperialist policy of aggression and invasion, but also promoted peace in the Far East and other parts of the world. Now times have changed. An epochal transformation has occurred in the global scene. A return to the 1950s-type alliance would not only run counter to the interests of the Chinese and Soviet people, but also go against the current world trend.

Similarly, a return to the inter-party relations of the 1950s would be out of the question. The big party mentality on the part of the Communist Party of the Soviet Union had led to such abnormal practices as unequal treatment of other parties, and a monopoly of the final say on theoretical matters and the like in the past. All these had affected and impaired mutual relations between the Soviet and the Chinese communist parties. In his speech at a May 17, 1989 press conference in Beijing, Soviet General Secretary Mikhail Gorbachev appropriately summarised the experience in this respect by pointing out that the inter-party relationship should be one of equality and cooperation based on mutual respect for one another's viewpoints and experience, and non-interference in internal affairs. He described this as a lesson learned from untold bitterness and suffering. A logical conclusion to be derived from this summing up of the past is that there can be no return to the alliance of the 1950s.

Another issue of widespread concern is whether the Sino-Soviet normalisation will harm the interests of any third country. The Sino-Soviet joint communique has declared in unequivocal terms that 'the normalisation of Sino-Soviet relations is not directed at any third country, nor does it harm its interests'.

China adheres to an independent foreign policy of peace, and is resolute in opposing hegemonism and defending world peace. Seeking alliances with any country would not only violate this principle of maintaining independence but would also be detrimental to world peace. Although an economically weak, developing country, China is, after all, a major power with a huge population and a vast territory, enjoying considerable influence in international relations. Guided by the policies of reform and opening up to the outside world, China is pushing ahead with its four modernisations drive to eliminate poverty and backwardness. Realisation of the national dream of strength and prosperity would be unthinkable without a peaceful international environment, and would require sustained efforts of several generations and peaceful construction lasting decades or even hundreds of years.

The Sino-Soviet normalisation together with relaxation of tensions along the border areas is favourable for China to build good neighbourly relations with other nearby countries. With Sino-Soviet normalisation, Sino-Mongolian relations are also moving toward rapprochement with restoration of normal intercourse and a noticeable advance in economic and political fields. Sino-Indian relations have likewise registered some initial improvement. Along with a political settlement to the Cambodian issue and Hanoi's abandonment of its policy of aggression against Cambodia and opposition to China, Sino-Vietnamese normalisation might be put on the agenda. All these would benefit China's domestic construction.

Following Sino-Soviet normalisation, some alterations may come about in Moscow's relations with other Asia-Pacific countries. However, insofar as China is concerned, friendly relations with all countries including the United States will be maintained and, if possible, expanded. At present, Sino-US relations are developing steadily to the satisfaction of both sides. Yet some obstacles persist. Only by seeking solutions to them in strict accordance with the principles defined in the three joint communiques between the two countries, coupled with faithful fulfilment of promises made by the US administration, will it be possible to ensure stable and sustained development of Sino-US relations. Since ancient times, there have always been intimate contacts and a profound friendship between the people of China and its close neighbour Japan. The four principles of peace and friendship, equality and mutual benefit, mutual trust, and long-term stability form the basis for the development of bilateral relations between China and Japan. Although frictions over some political and economic issues do occur between the two sides, with mutual understanding and appropriate handling, it is possible for the Chinese and Japanese to maintain their friendly and harmonious relations from generation to generation. Despite certain misunderstandings between China and some members of the Association of Southeast Asian Nations (Asean) on some issues, traditional friendship prevails. Facts speak louder than words. With the passing of time, mutual understanding and trust are bound to develop. On China's part, careful attention and strenuous effort has always been given to forging a closer and deeper friendship with the Asean countries.

It can thus be assumed that China will intensify its diplomatic activities in pursuit of warmer friendships with all the other countries, while fostering goodwill with the Soviet Union. However, if China should seek amity with a given country at the expense of any third country, it would violate the principled position of its external policy and be rejected by the Chinese public.

Overall, Sino-Soviet normalisation will benefit peace and development in the Asia-Pacific region.

Firstly, it will facilitate a gradual defusing of military confrontation in this vast region. Moscow has begun to withdraw a large number of troops from Mongolia in the wake of the Afghanistan pullout and plans to reduce its troops along the Sino-Soviet border. Gorbachev has also announced a reduction in troop strength of 120,000 in the Soviet Far East and the removal of 16 warships from the Soviet Pacific fleet. With growing international detente, the momentum of the arms race will gradually slow down even though there is yet no major alteration in the US-Soviet strategic confrontation in this part of the world. However, some countries are still engaged in arms expansion. No matter what motives they may have, such action does not harmonise with the current global trend of detente and demands our attention.

Secondly, it will shift the focus towards the economic race among the Asia-Pacific countries where economic diplomacy will play an increasingly important role in international relations. Since the advent of the 1980s, the rapid emergence of the Asia-Pacific as a regional economic power has attracted worldwide attention. While the region commanded only a 10 per cent share in total world GNP in the 1960s, the figure has jumped to 20 per cent in 1988. Over the past decade and more, the growth rate of the Asia-Pacific economy has been higher than that of other parts of the world and the region holds promise of becoming the economic centre of the world in the next century.

For some time to come, the United States and Japan will continue to play a dominant role in the Asia-Pacific regional economy, a basic fact which should not be ignored in sizing up the situation. Economically, most Asia-Pacific countries still rely to a large extent on the United States for both export trade and investment, with the region recording a 36 per cent share of total US foreign trade and 14 per cent of total US overseas investment in 1988. Conversely, the

Asia-Pacific is likewise indispensable to the US with its trade volume with the US surpassing that of Western Europe's.

Japan, the mainstay in the regional economy and a world economic power, is economically interdependent with the United States, a fact tied to the two countries' mutual reliance for survival and their raging competition. Japan is now vying with the US in expanding economic relations with the 'four dragons' (Singapore, South Korea, Hongkong and Taiwan) and the other Asean countries with its trade with these economies accounting for over 20 per cent of its total exports. Accumulative figures in a 1986 year-end survey show that close to 20 per cent of Japanese private direct investments and half of Tokyo's official economic aid went to these Asian economies.

Conceivably, the direction of this US-Japan partnership of cooperation and competition will be a crucial factor in affecting the prospects for Asia-Pacific economic cooperation.

The Soviet Union is also seeking an active role in Asia-Pacific economic cooperation by acting upon Gorbachev's 'new thinking in foreign policy' in the form of gradual alleviation of regional military confrontation, expanded interaction with other regional economies and exploitation of the Soviet Far East. But it would take time for Moscow to revert its political passivity and economic weakness in this region.

China is in a position to foster economic complementarity with many other regional countries, considering its vast size, significant political influence, huge market potential and abundant supply of labour. But its relative economic weakness has predetermined that China could not turn into a powerful competitor for other regional economies.

It thus appears that a variety of forms of bilateral or multi-lateral economic cooperation better suits Asia-Pacific realities given its diversity in economic levels, social systems, economic models, political inclination and national cultures, together with a complicated interlocking of interests and contradictions, a mosaic not to be seen elsewhere in the world. It would seem to be more practicable to form some loose organisation for economic cooperation on a mixed bilateral and multi-lateral basis. The concept of a comparatively unified and tight-knit economic community will perhaps have to wait for a number of years until conditions are suitable.

Under these circumstances, China will stick to its policies of reform and opening up to the outside world and seek closer economic contacts with other Asia-Pacific countries while speeding up its own national construction. At the same time, China will make due contribution to common development and economic prosperity of the Asia-Pacific region through active participation in region-wide economic cooperation and technological exchange, by filling up each other's deficiencies and helping supply each other's needs in accordance with the principles of equality and mutual benefit.

A new stage in Sino-Soviet relations

GENNADY I CHUFRIN

Head of department, Institute of Oriental Studies, Academy of Science, USSR

MIKHAIL GORBACHEV'S visit to China in the middle of May, 1989 has become an important event in Sino-Soviet relations as well as in the more general context of Asia-Pacific and global politics. This visit symbolised the end of three decades of Sino-Soviet animosity, effectively normalised interstate relations between China and the USSR, and restored party-to-party relations between the two largest communist parties in the world. All these results of Gorbachev's visit are well known and have received extensive coverage in the world press. Therefore I shall not in this paper concentrate on the visit as a separate, though admittedly politically most important, event in present Sino-Soviet relatons but shall attempt to analyse these relations in retrospective as well as in perspective.

Sino-Soviet normalisation is not a single dramatic event but a gradual, lengthy process which has been going on between China and the USSR for almost a decade with ups and downs, successes and failures. This process obviously did not start with Gorbachev's visit to Beijing, neither is it completely over. In spite of the overall Sino-Soviet normalisation a number of differences have yet to be resolved. This has been noted by many observers and analysts of international relations and quite a few scenarios of possible results of Sino-Soviet normalisation and their impact on Sino-Soviet bilateral as well as international relations have been cited in the press. I would like to contribute to this analytical process and suggest my own perception of what the Sino-Soviet normalisation means to us and to the outside world.

In this connection I would like to start with a statement that by the end of the 1970s, Sino-Soviet relations had reached their lowest level which was not only undesirable from the Soviet point of view but objectively created a situation in the Asia-Pacific area which was insecure and potentially dangerous for regional countries. Therefore the Soviet leadership stated its intentions to change the situation radically, to dispel possible fears of China with regard to perceived Soviet intentions in the Asia-Pacific region and to improve our bilateral relations with China. This policy was further developed when Gorbachev became the leader of the Soviet Union and was articulated by him in a number of foreign policy statements, the best known being his speeches at the 27th Party Congress in February 1986, in Vladivostok in July 1986 and in Krasnoyarsk in September 1988.

The Chinese leadership, governed by their own national as well as international modalities, responded rather favourably to Soviet proposals aimed at normalisation. This important change in Chinese attitude towards the Soviet Union was, in my opinion, motivated by the overall change in Chinese international behaviour, which was characterised by the shift from the policy of strategic cooperation with the United States towards the policy of equidistance between the superpowers. Obviously this change of policy was made by China in its own national interests but it created at the same time a favourable climate for the normalisation of Sino-Soviet relations. However the Chinese leadership put forward a number of preconditions for such a normalisation which have become widely, though not very correctly, known as 'three obstacles'.

This gesture was understood by many Soviet analysts to be a sign of Chinese desire to proceed with the normalisation process — but at a controlled speed regulated from Beijing. However, since at least two of those 'obstacles' were not in the nature of bilateral Sino-Soviet relations, their 'removal' could not possibly be done according to Chinese wishes. Thus the Soviet policy towards the Afghanistan crisis and the withdrawal of Soviet troops from Afghanistan were implemented in accordance with the best interests of the Soviet Union as they are understood by the Soviet leadership and certainly not under Chinese pressure. Similarly, the Kampuchean problem started to settle down not because of some dramatic Soviet moves but because the Khmer factions themselves decided to resolve their differences through the political process on the principles of national reconciliation, while Vietnam announced the timetable of its troops' withdrawal from Kampuchea.

At the same time the Soviet Union displayed its readiness to discuss and resolve those problems that indeed constituted part of bilateral Sino-Soviet relations. Most prominent among them were the problems of demarcation of the Sino-Soviet border and its demilitarisation. In his Vladivostok speech Gorbachev suggested certain concrete steps to resolve those problems including the demarcation of the border along the main shipping channel of the Amur river. It was announced simultaneously that as a gesture of goodwill a substantial part of Soviet troops would be withdrawn from Mongolia in consultation with the Mongolian leadership. In fact the Soviet Union has since 1985 started to reduce its armed forces in the Soviet Far East and taken a unilateral obligation not to increase its nuclear potential here.

When the Soviet-American Intermediate-range Nuclear Forces (INF) treaty was signed, the USSR agreed to liquidate 436 shorter and medium range missiles in the eastern part of the country. The next step taken by the USSR in the context of demilitarisation of the Far East will be reduction of Soviet troops by 120,000 men during 1989-90. During his visit to Beijing Gorbachev also announced that the Soviet Union had started another substantial reduction of its armed forces in Mongolia which will bring down the total strength of the Soviet army there by 75 per cent.

All these steps combined are meant to change radically the situation in the Far East and particularly on the Sino-Soviet border down to its complete demilitarisation. Although this target has not so far been fully achieved, it was stated in the joint communique during Gorbachev's visit to Beijing that both sides agreed 'to take measures in order to reduce armed forces in the region of the Sino-Soviet border to a minimum level which would conform to the normal relations of good neighbours'. As for the border talks, during the last three rounds of negotiations, a substantial progress has been already achieved on the major part of the eastern Sino-Soviet border while consultations on the eastern part of the border have begun. To facilitate the border talks the Soviet and Chinese sides exchanged the appropriate aerial photomaterials, an unthinkable event even a few years ago.

Another important sphere of Sino-Soviet relations where substantial progress has been achieved during the last few years is in bilateral trade and economic relations. In 1983, for instance, the volume of this trade was less than 0.5 billion roubles. In 1988 it reached 1.85 billion roubles, thus registering an annual growth rate of around 30 per cent. About 30 to 40 per cent of Soviet exports to China consist of machinery and equipment, most important among them being power equipment, cars, aircraft, railway rolling stock and electrical equipment. Besides these, the Soviet Union sells to China ferrous and non-ferrous metals, timber, fertilizers and other chemical goods and a number of consumption goods. In return the Soviet Union imports from China a wide range of commodities, including textiles, shoes, clothes, various electronic goods, food and raw materials.

This bilateral trade which is carried out within the legal framework of the interstate long-range agreement signed by the governments of the USSR and China on July 10, 1985, is supplemented by the Sino-Soviet frontier trade which was resumed in 1983 and which has since increased from 6.3 million roubles to over 100 million roubles. The frontier trade includes fertilizers, construction materials and agricultural implements as well as such durable consumption goods as refrigerators, dry-cleaners, washing machines and motorcycles from the Soviet side with meat, fruit, textiles and shoes from the Chinese side.

The Soviet Union and China have also signed a number of contracts envisaging the upgrading of a number of Chinese industrial enterprises with Soviet as well as Chinese participation in building hotels and roads in the Soviet Far East. The Soviet-Chinese commission on economic, trade and scientific cooperation which was established in 1985 plays an important role in developing trade and economic relations between the two countries. Under the purview of this commission are various forms of such cooperation as joint ventures and promotion of direct links between Soviet and Chinese enterprises, transfers of technology and buyback trade.

As a result of these developments the Soviet Union has now become the fifth biggest trading partner of China, although the volume of Soviet-Chinese trade lags behind the volume of Chinese trade with Hong Kong, the United States or Japan. Both the Soviet Union and China may get additional advantages out of further development of their trade and economic relations. Mutually advantageous cooperation between the two countries may be used, for instance, for the priority development of power production in China and an agro-industrial complex in the Soviet Union. Taking into consideration that the Soviet Union now pays special attention to the development of its eastern regions and that China's interior provinces which lag behind the coastal provinces in their economic development need a stable foreign trading partner, both countries may further explore possibilities of frontier trade across the longest common border in the world.

Besides trade links the Soviet Union and China may further develop various forms of technical cooperation which is already carried out through Soviet participation in the construction and upgrading of 46 Chinese industrial projects. Another important sign of progress in the Sino-Soviet relations is the growing exchange of scholars, teachers and students between the two countries. In 1983, when student exchange was resumed after a lengthy interval, only 20 students were involved from both sides. By 1988 the number of Soviet students in China and Chinese students in the USSR increased to 450. Direct links between various universities and other higher educational institutions have been resumed since 1987 and now cover nine such institutions including Moscow and Beijing state universities and the Leningrad polytechnic institute. Besides, links are growing between Soviet and Chinese secondary schools which involve the expanding exchange of teachers, textbooks and other educational materials.

One of the major results of Mikhail Gorbachev's visit to China is the normalisation of relations between the Communist Party of the Soviet Union and the Communist Party of China. Both the Soviet *perestroika* and Chinese modernisation that created a new concept of socialism which the ruling parties of both countries are moving towards played a role in restoring inter-party relations. The joint communique signed in Beijing in May 1989 stated that the two communist parties will resume regular contacts and exchanges based on the principles of independence and sovereignty, complete equality, mutual respect and non-interference in each other's internal affairs. Although such a formula may sound a little bit too cautious with regard to the relations between the two largest communist parties in the world, nevertheless one cannot underestimate the significance of this agreement which puts an end to the sharp ideological confrontation between China and the Soviet Union during the last three decades.

In listing the major achievements in Sino-Soviet political, economic, ideological and other relations during the last decade or so, and especially during the last three to four years, it was not my intention to create a rosy picture. My task was, as I understood it, to show a substantial qualitative progress in these relations and to disabuse anyone from the notion that what has been achieved may be only of passing significance. At the same time it would be an impermissible exaggeration to present the present stage of Sino-Soviet relations as free from any differences or that, as a result of Mikhail Gorbachev's visit to Beijing and his talks with the top leaders, the relations between our countries are moving towards what they were in the 1950s when China and the USSR were military allies.

The most significant characteristic of the new stage in Sino-Soviet relations is that although both countries are socialist states, our relations are no longer based on ideology but on the universal principles of peaceful co-existence, mutual respect and non-interference in each other's domestic affairs. That means there should be not only more sober, business-like relations between the two countries that are at the same time both friendly and mutually advantageous, but also the development of Sino-Soviet relations should in no way reflect negatively on the existing relations of the Soviet Union or China with third countries.

It is only natural that under these circumstances approaches of the Soviet Union and China to difficult issues of international or domestic significance may be different. It is even more so in the case of public attitudes in the two countries towards such issues, which may be quite different from the official position. A recent case in point is the reserved and formal attitude of the Soviet government towards the Tiananmen events and a very emotional negative response of the Soviet public towards them. This should be accepted by the Chinese leadership as clear manifestation of political pluralism in the Soviet Union and not interpreted in any other way.

Having stated this, I nevertheless would like to suggest that there is a clear possibility in growing parallelism of Soviet and Chinese approaches in future to various international problems (for instance, international economic reforms, reduction of nuclear war threat, resolution of various regional conflicts, etc) because of similarity of views between our countries on many of these issues. This similarity of views was reflected in the joint communique signed in Beijing. I do not believe that this may be seen as a cause for any worry for other countries. I would interpret this similarity of views only as a healthy sign of increasing responsibility assumed by the Soviet Union and China for promoting international stability and security in the name of development and prosperity.

Admittedly the same communique reflected the still existing differences in opinions between the USSR and China on some of the important international issues (for instance, the Kampuchean problem). But it is my firm opinion that these differences should not be allowed to grow into 'obstacles' since such a scenario is neither in the interest of China nor the Soviet Union, not is it in the best interests of other countries in the Asia-Pacific region.

Soviet-Japanese relations in the short, medium and long term

PEGGY FALKENHEIM
Professor of Political Science, University of Western Ontario, London, Canada

Introduction

IN THE more than four years since Mikhail Gorbachev's accession to power, the USSR has achieved major breakthroughs in relations with China, West Germany, the United States and other long term adversaries. These breakthroughs have been made possible by Moscow's adoption of a new foreign policy approach, placing greater emphasis on mutual security and cooperative efforts to resolve global problems. As part of this new approach, the USSR has made a number of significant foreign policy changes, *viz*, withdrawing troops from Afghanistan and Mongolia, working toward the resolution of regional conflicts in Indochina and elsewhere, and agreeing to on-site inspection and other terms facilitating arms control agreements. This new foreign policy approach and the accompanying domestic political and economic reforms have produced a marked change in foreign popular perceptions of Soviet intentions and a slower and more grudging, albeit increasingly significant, shift in elite views. These changes now seem to hold out the promise of a radical transformation away from cold war relations to what President George Bush has recently referred to as the post-containment era.

In contrast to this positive trend, Soviet-Japanese relations have experienced relatively little movement. The Gorbachev leadership has increased efforts to woo Japan but they have produced few significant changes in Soviet-Japanese relations which are stalemated by an unresolved territorial dispute and opposing

Soviet and Japanese security concerns. This stalemate worries the Gorbachev leadership because improved Soviet relations with Japan are necessary to support efforts to develop the Soviet Far East and East Siberia, to integrate the Soviet economy with other Asia-Pacific economies, and to reduce regional tensions.

The purpose of this paper is to analyse both the bilateral problems creating a Soviet-Japanese stalemate and the broader global and regional trends which will have an important bearing on their relations. It will argue that positive trends in the global and regional international environments are likely to have a favourable impact on Soviet-Japanese relations.

Gorbachev's Japan policy

Under Gorbachev, the Soviet leadership recognises that improved relations with Japan are important if the Soviet Union is to achieve its goals of developing its Far Eastern regions and gaining acceptance as a legitimate participant in Asian international affairs.[1] This increasing Soviet awareness of Japan's importance was reflected in Gorbachev's July 28, 1986 Vladivostok speech in which he called Japan 'a power of paramount importance' and in his September 1988 Krasnoyarsk speech in which he devoted even more attention to Japan. In a May 1989 speech in Beijing, Gorbachev departed from his prepared text to call for 'full-blooded' relations with Japan.

In an effort to improve Soviet relations with Japan, the Gorbachev leadership has increased the number and range of diplomatic contacts. Since January 1986, the foreign ministers of the USSR and Japan have met four times for formal consultations in addition to their meetings at the United Nations, the chemical weapons' talks in Paris and other fora. In the eight preceding years, there had been informal meetings but no formal consultations between the foreign ministers largely because former Soviet Foreign Minister Andrei Gromyko was reluctant to confront Japanese demands for the return of the northern islands, territories claimed by Japan but occupied by the Soviet Union.

Gorbachev has expressed a willingness to visit Japan. Although this visit has been postponed a number of times, when Gorbachev goes to Japan, his visit will be of great symbolic importance because it will be the first time that a top Soviet leader has ever visited that country. To foster better relations with Tokyo, Moscow has made changes in foreign policy personnel by appointing a Japanese-speaking career foreign service professional as ambassador to Tokyo and removing hard-liner Ivan Kovalenko from his party Central Committee post in charge of Japan policy.

In an effort to woo Japan, the Gorbachev leadership has adopted a more

1. For a more detailed analysis of recent changes in Soviet policies toward Japan, see the author's 'Evolving regional ties in Northeast Asia: Japan, the US and the USSR,' *Asian Survey*, 28:12 (December 1988), pp 1229-44.

flexible attitude toward the territorial dispute. The USSR has lifted a requirement, imposed from 1976-86, that Japanese citizens visiting their relatives' graves on the disputed territory have valid passports and Soviet visas. This requirement had led to a suspension of visits to the graves because Japan's Foreign Ministry was concerned that compliance with it would imply recognition of Soviet sovereignty over the disputed islands.

In contrast to previous Soviet efforts to deny the existence of a territorial dispute, the Gorbachev leadership has at least implicitly acknowledged its existence and agreed to discuss it. During Foreign Minister Eduard Shevardnadze's December 1988 talks with Foreign Minister Sosuke Uno in Tokyo, the two sides agreed to establish a working group to negotiate the terms for a peace treaty.[2] The joint communique issued at the end of Shevardnadze's visit contained an elliptical reference to the territorial dispute. Two meetings of the working group have been held since then at which the Soviet and Japanese participants have each set forth their quite different interpretations of the historical record, bolstering their opposing claims to the northern territories.

There have been hints that the Gorbachev leadership might consider making some concessions on the substance of the territorial dispute. On several occasions, the Gorbachev leadership has intimated that it would be willing to return two of the disputed islands, the Habomais and Shikotan, to Japan.[3]

The Gorbachev leadership is trying to attract Japanese trade and investment to help develop the Soviet Far East and East Siberia and to support Soviet efforts to raise industrial productivity, modernise industry and promote conservation. To encourage the expansion of Soviet economic ties with Japan and other capitalist countries, the Gorbachev leadership has adopted new policies decentralising the management of foreign trade, allowing the creation of joint ventures on Soviet soil and liberalising the rules governing them. Tax breaks have been offered to foreign investors, including special tax breaks to encourage investment in the Soviet Far East. The Soviet Union has announced its intention to establish special economic zones to attract foreign investment, at least one or two of which are expected to be located in the Soviet Far East.[4] To relieve

---

2.   Two other working groups were established to discuss other Soviet-Japanese bilateral issues and Asia-Pacific affairs.

3.   Mainichi Daily News, May 8, 1988 and Yomiuri, August 4, 1988, p2 in Daily Summary of the Japanese Press, August 19, 1989, pp 8-9. These hints were made during Gorbachev's May 1988 meeting with Takako Doi, Chairperson of the Japan Socialist Party, and during his July 1988 meeting with former Japanese Prime Minister Nakasone.

4.   Sophie Quinn-Judge, 'Partners preferred: Moscow moves to strengthen links with Pacific Region,' Far Eastern Economic Review, February 2, 1989, p54 and Sophie Quinn-Judge, 'A model for reform,' Far Eastern Economic Review, May 25, 1989, p16. As of April 1, 1989, any state or cooperative enterprise is allowed to engage in direct negotiations with a foreign partner without prior governmental permission. Foreigners are allowed to own more than 50 per cent of a joint venture's equity and to control its management.

congestion caused by bottlenecks in Soviet ports, Moscow has enlisted Japanese help to expand the cargo handling facilities at its Far Eastern port of Vostochnyy and has promised to allow foreign merchant ships to use Vladivostok and Vanino in addition to Nakhodka and Vostochnyy.[5]

In changes aimed even more at China than at Japan, Gorbachev has taken steps to reduce military tensions in the Asia-Pacific region. In the intermediate nuclear forces accord, the Gorbachev leadership bowed to pressure from Japan, China and other countries and agreed to eliminate its land-based intermediate and short-range nuclear missiles from Asia as well as from Europe. After Gorbachev's July 28, 1986 Vladivostok speech, the Soviet Union removed one division of troops from Mongolia. In his December 1988 United Nations speech and his May 1989 speech in Beijing, Gorbachev promised to withdraw the remaining Soviet troops from Mongolia, to reduce the Soviet armed forces by 500,000 men — 200,000 of whom will be withdrawn from Asia — and to scrap 10,000 tanks, 8,500 guns and 800 combat aircraft. In Beijing, Gorbachev announced that 120,000 of these troops would be cut from forces deployed in the Soviet Far East and that 16 vessels would be scrapped from the Soviet Pacific fleet.

Gorbachev has made an unprecedented number of regional arms control proposals. He has advocated a wide variety of measures, among them confidence building measures such as advance notification of and limitations on the size and location of military exercises, the creation of nuclear free zones and other limitations on the deployment, testing and proliferation of nuclear weapons, restrictions on naval weapons and activities and on anti-submarine warfare, the removal of foreign bases from the Asia-Pacific region and the dissolution of military alliances. The Gorbachev leadership has reiterated Soviet arms control proposals directed by previous Soviet leaderships specifically at Japan, among them a proposal that the Soviet Union guarantee not to launch a nuclear attack on Japan in return for a Japanese commitment to strictly enforce its three non-nuclear principles barring the production or possession of nuclear weapons or their introduction into Japanese territory.[6]

Soviet-Japanese territorial stalemate

While producing some limited improvement in Soviet-Japanese relations, Gorbachev's policies have so far not succeeded in ending the stalemate. Soviet territorial concessions have not gone far enough to satisfy Japanese demands. Ja-

---

5.   *Mainichi Daily News*, April 20, 1989, p7. However, there is no indication when these ports would be open to foreign commerce.

6.   Soviet motivations for these proposals and the Japanese and US reactions to them are analysed in Peggy L Falkenheim, 'Obstacles to regional arms control in Northeast Asia,' in *Peace and Security in the Asia-Pacific Region* (Canberra: Australian National University, 1989), ed Andrew Mack.

pan's Foreign Ministry insists that the conclusion of a peace treaty should be made conditional upon Moscow's agreement to return Kunashiri and Etorofu, as well as the Habomais and Shikotan. Hints of Soviet willingness to return two of the four disputed islands are not seen by Foreign Ministry Soviet specialists as a meaningful concession since they do not go beyond concessions made by Moscow in the 1956 Joint Declaration, more than 30 years ago.

To bolster its territorial position, the Japanese government has been soliciting international support. Last summer, the British government, one of the signatories of the Yalta pact, issued a statement endorsing Japan's interpretation of the historical record.[7] The United States has expressed support for Japan's territorial demands, most recently in the May 1989 speech by President Bush at Texas A&M University.

So far, there is no sign that Moscow is willing to accept Japan's demand for the return of all four islands. Moscow justifies its position both on historical grounds and with the argument that altering the territorial boundaries established by World War II would create a dangerous precedent.[8] This precedent could be particularly dangerous now that Moscow confronts territorial demands not only from other countries but also from minority nationalities within its own borders eager to revise internal territorial boundaries or, in the case of the Baltic republics, to reverse the results of World War II by seceding from the USSR.

As an added obstacle, the northern territories are of strategic significance. Possession of them makes it easier for the Soviet Union to control the entrances and exits to the Sea of Okhotsk, one of the two main sea bastions for the deployment of Soviet strategic nuclear missile carrying submarines. The main logistical supply route to the Soviet naval base at Petropavlovsk passes through waters close to the northern territories.

Last summer and fall, Soviet academic specialists on Japan advocated compromise solutions which they hoped would overcome the gap between the positions of the two governments. Various possibilities, suggested at seminars and in private conversations, included the return of two islands and the establishment of a free economic zone on the other two, the return of the Habomais and Shikotan and joint sovereignty over Kunashiri and Etorofu (the Spitzbergen method) and postponing consideration of the dispute and allowing future generations to resolve it, as Japan has done in its territorial dispute with China over the Senkaku islands. Although some of these academic specialists are known to have close ties to the Gorbachev leadership, it is not clear if they were floating trial balloons with official approval or acting on their own initiative because they recognise the importance of finding a way out of this impasse.

---

7.   Hiroshi Kimura 'Gorbachev and the Northern Territories,' *Voice*, October 1988, pp 112-22, in *Japan Echo*, 15:4 (Winter 1988), p20.

8.   When Gorbachev made this argument in his July 1988 meeting with Nakasone, the former Japanese Prime Minister replied that considerations of this kind had not stopped the United States from returning Okinawa, an island whose capture had cost so many American lives.

In recent months, Soviet officials and articles in the Soviet press have been advocating the Senkakus formula that Japan and the USSR should postpone resolution of the territorial dispute until a future generation.[9] In a lecture given at the time of his December 1988 visit to Japan, Shevardnadze urged the Japanese not to 'hold all other matters hostage' to the resolution of the territorial issue.[10] In a May 1989 meeting with then Foreign Minister Uno, Gorbachev suggested that the Soviet Union and Japan should shelve the territorial dispute as Japan and China have done in their dispute over the Senkakus and Japan and South Korea have done in their dispute over Takeshima.[11] In a November 1989 press conference in Tokyo, Aleksandr Yakovlev, one of Gorbachev's top foreign policy advisers, hinted at the possibility of a 'third way' of resolving the territorial dispute. When asked for clarification of his remarks, Yakovlev said that he favoured the deepening and expansion of Soviet-Japanese relations to create better 'mutual trust, understanding and respect' which would make it easier to resolve existing problems. While Yakovlev's original comment was seen as a hint that Moscow was contemplating a territorial concession, his clarification can be interpreted as support for postponing resolution of the territorial dispute.[12]

If the trial balloons last summer and fall were meant to elicit an acceptable compromise solution, then the recent emphasis on the Senkakus formula may reflect the failure to find one. Alternatively, Moscow may be stalling out of a conviction that it is not worth dealing with a Japanese leadership badly weakened by the Recruit scandal. A weak leadership is less likely to be able to offer Moscow meaningful concessions on credit, trade and other matters in return for a territorial concession.

Economic relations

The failure to resolve the territorial dispute has negatively affected Japan's attitude toward economic relations with the USSR. Tokyo is pursuing a policy of 'not separating economics from politics' by refusing to conclude a long-term economic cooperation agreement with the USSR or an investment guarantee pact or to extend government credits until the territorial dispute has been resolved. Japan's Foreign Ministry is determined to use whatever leverage it has available and not to repeat the mistakes made in the early 1970s when some

---

9.   See, for example, Moscow Television Service in Russian, December 18, 1988, Commentary by Vsevolod Ovchinnikov, *Foreign Broadcast Information Service: Soviet Union*, No 245 (December 21, 1988), p19.

10.   Tokyo, NHK General Television Network in Japanese, December 20, 1988 in *Foreign Broadcast Information Service: Soviet Union*, No 246 (December 22, 1988), p7.

11.   *Mainichi Daily News*, May 7, 1989, p1.

12.   *Asahi Shimbun*, November 16, 1989, p2, translation in *Daily Summary of the Japanese Press*, November 21, 1989, p7.

analysts believe Japan lost an opportunity to resolve the territorial dispute at a time when the Soviet Union was eager to forestall a Sino-Japanese rapprochement. By agreeing too quickly at that time to establish diplomatic relations with China and to initiate Siberian development projects funded by government credits, Japan is thought by some to have reduced its leverage over the USSR.

Japan's policy of not separating economics from politics has impeded Soviet efforts to attract Japanese trade and investment. Another obstacle has been Cocom (the Coordinating Committee for Multilateral Export Controls) restrictions on the sale of militarily useful relevant high technology to the USSR which have been applied more strictly in Japan since the 1987 Toshiba scandal. However, economic rather than political factors have been the main barriers to an expansion of Soviet-Japanese economic ties. One obstacle is the trade imbalance in Japan's favour and the limited range of attractive Soviet goods available for export to Japan. Successful conservation efforts in Japan and an increasing emphasis on knowledge-intensive as opposed to resource-intensive industry have limited Japanese demand for Soviet energy and raw materials. Japanese firms have found alternative sources of supply for energy and raw materials which for both economic and political reasons are more attractive than the USSR. Even with economic reform, it is unlikely that the Soviet Union in the foreseeable future will be able to produce a significant quantity of attractive manufactured goods for export to Japan. Moscow's ability to pay for Japanese products is limited by the yen's appreciation and by the declining price of oil and natural gas, two principal Soviet exports which affect the USSR's hard currency reserves.

Despite the recent changes in the Soviet joint venture law, Japanese and other foreign investors still face a number of serious obstacles. The rouble's lack of convertibility makes it difficult to repatriate profits.[13] The unavailability or unreliability of supplies impedes joint venture operations. Japanese investors face a very poor physical and social infrastructure in the Soviet Far East and Siberia which makes foreign investment in these regions less attractive for Japan than it is for West European investors in the European part of the USSR or for Japanese investors in other parts of Asia. Unlike China and other prospective Japanese joint venture partners, Siberia and the Soviet Far East lack a plentiful supply of relatively cheap labour.

So far, the USSR has had only limited success in attracting Japanese investment. Approximately 20 relatively small scale Soviet-Japanese joint ventures have been established, mostly in the fields of lumber and fish processing, and restaurant, tourist and sports facilities. Besides these bilateral ventures, Japanese firms are participating with US and European firms in at least three tri- or multi-

---

13. The Soviet government has indicated its intention to devalue the rouble by 50 per cent for commercial transactions by January 1990, to establish a single commercial exchange rate by 1991 and eventually to make the rouble convertible. However, the obstacles to making the rouble convertible are considered to be so great that it is not expected that it will happen soon.

lateral ventures for the construction of large petrochemical plants in the USSR.[14] While these joint ventures are not insignificant, they constitute only a small proportion of the more than 1,000 joint ventures already registered in the USSR.

Military tensions

Tensions created by the Soviet military buildup in the region around Japan are an important factor behind the continued Soviet-Japanese stalemate. Japanese defence planners have observed that despite Gorbachev's talk about military reductions, the modernisation of Soviet Far East air and naval forces has continued. The Soviet Pacific fleet included some of the USSR's modern vessels including two Kiev class carriers, Delta III and Delta IV class SSBNs[15], new, quieter Akula class attack submarines, Sovremenny and Udaloy class guided missile destroyers and Ivan Rogov class amphibious ships. To counter the West's F-15 fighters, the USSR has deployed in the Far East more than 100 fourth generation MiG-31 Foxhound and Sukhoi-27 Flankers with extended flight ranges and superior firearms' control capabilities. The Flankers are equipped with infrared-ray bombing site equipment capable of pointing missiles at a target without emitting radar waves. This equipment makes it possible for them to launch an attack without the other side being aware of it. Deployment of these long-range fighters to the Far East has the effect of extending the range of the Soviet strategic Badger and Bear bombers which they accompany to cover all of Japan.[16] The Soviet Union also deploys approximately 85 Backfire bombers armed with air-to-ground and air-to-ship missiles capable of attacking ground targets in Japan and the surrounding sea lanes.[17]

The Gorbachev leadership has rejected demands that it reduce its military deployments in the disputed northern territories. An army division is deployed there armed with 130mm long-range guns capable of hitting Hokkaido, MiG-24 Hind attack helicopters, approximately 45 MiG-23 Flogger fighters and ground

14.   One multilateral venture involving Occidental Petroleum, Montedison of Italy and Marubeni Corporation is studying the feasibility of establishing a US$5 billion petrochemical complex at Tengiz, near the Caspian Sea. Mitsubishi, Mitsui and Chiyoda in cooperation with a US firm Combustion Engineering are studying the feasibility of constructing a US$5 billion petrochemical complex at Nizhnevartovsk in West Siberia. (Charles Smith, 'Making raw deals: Narrowly based Japanese-Soviet trade may have peaked,' *Far Eastern Economic Review*, December 22, 1988, pp 28-29). Another petrochemical venture, involving Combustion Engineering as the lead firm and Mitsubishi and Mitsui, is exploring the possibility of constructing a petrochemical plant at Surgut in West Siberia. (*Mainichi Daily News*, January 5, 1989 and April 6, 1989, p12).

15.   *Sankei*, September 17, 1988, p1 in *Daily Summary of the Japanese Press*, September 29, 1989, p12.

16.   *Nihon Keizai*, January 1, 1989, p3 in *Daily Summary of the Japanese Press*, January 10, 1989, p10 and *Sankei*, Eve, December 26, 1988, p1 in *Daily Summary of the Japanese Press*, January 4, 1989, pp 11-12.

17.   *Sankei*, September 17, 1988, p1 in *Daily Summary of the Japanese Press*, September 29, 1989, p12.

launched cruise missiles capable of carrying nuclear warheads.[18] In addition, it was revealed in October 1988 that Soviet military deployments in the Sea of Okhotsk area were increased by the redeployment to Sakhalin of an attack helicopter unit from Afghanistan armed with approximately 60 helicopters of various types including the new, powerful Hind D-type helicopter which could pose a threat to Hokkaido.[19]

Besides modernising its own East Asian forces, the USSR has been increasing security cooperation with North Korea and selling it more advanced arms. In recent years, Moscow has sold Pyongyang SU-25 Frogfoot attack aircraft, MiG-29 Fulcrum fighters and the long range SA-5/Gammon surface-to-air missile system.[20] For three consecutive years from the fall of 1986 through the fall of 1988, Soviet and North Korean forces have conducted joint exercises. It is interesting to note that in 1988 these exercises were on a smaller scale than the previous year, perhaps to avoid undermining Soviet efforts to woo South Korean business partners.[21] In return for this increased security cooperation with Pyongyang, Soviet vessels have been granted access to the North Korean ports of Wonsan and Nampo, and Soviet planes have been granted the right to fly over North Korean airspace on their way to Indochina which enables them to expand their surveillance of Chinese, American and Japanese military activities.

Although there has been some decrease in Soviet Pacific naval deployments, this decrease has been more than offset by an increase in Soviet air activity. There has been an increase in the number of simulated strike missions flown by Soviet planes against Japan, Alaska and the Aleutians.[22] In fiscal 1988 (ending March 31, 1989), there was a 10 per cent increase in comparison with the previous fiscal year in the number of times Japanese planes had to scramble to meet unidentified aircraft approaching Japanese territory. On a number of occasions, Soviet planes engaged in zigzag attack training flights in which they charged straight at a radar site in Japan, made a reverse turn and then took aim at another radar site. While such training flights were not new, they were carried out more boldly and covered more sites than in previous years.[23]

Faced with this evidence of continued Soviet force modernisation, Japanese

---

18. Denis Warner, 'No change in Soviet military buildup,' *Pacific Defence Reporter*, March 1989, pp 40-41; *Mainichi Daily News*, January 15, 1989.

19. *Sankei*, October 21, 1988, p1 in *Daily Summary of the Japanese Press*, October 25, 1988, p14.

20. Admiral Ronald J Hays, 'The CINCPAC assessment,' *PDR (Pacific Defence Reporter) 1989 Annual Reference Edition*, 15: 6-7 (December 1988-January 1989), p8.

21. *Sankei*, November 7, 1988, p1 in *Daily Summary of the Japanese Press*, November 10, 1988, p11.

22. Admiral Ronald J Hays, 'The CINCPAC assessment,' *PDR (Pacific Defence Reporter) 1989 Annual Reference Edition*, 15: 6-7 (December 1988-January 1989), p14.

23. *Sankei*, Eve, December 26, 1988, p1 in *Daily Summary of the Japanese Press*, January 4, 1989, pp 11-12.

officials have reacted cautiously to Gorbachev's regional arms control proposals and to recent announcements of planned unilateral reductions in Soviet forces and weapons. Gorbachev's regional arms control proposals are perceived mostly as one-sided attempts to improve the position of the USSR at the expense of the United States and its allies. Japan has adopted a negative attitude toward them, in part because of a deep-seated mistrust of Soviet intentions and in part because Soviet proposals to remove foreign military bases from the Asia-Pacific region and to dissolve alliances would undermine Japan's security relationship with the United States upon which Japan depends for its defence. Soviet-proposed limits on anti-submarine warfare and naval armaments could impede efforts to modernise the Japanese armed forces. Negotiations on restricting naval nuclear armaments could prove embarrassing for the Japanese government by making it harder to pretend that US vessels entering Japanese ports do not carry nuclear weapons. Until the territorial dispute is resolved, Tokyo is reluctant to conclude an agreement on confidence building measures or any other pact with Moscow which Soviet leaders might see as an alternative to a peace treaty.

While Japanese defence analysts have welcomed recent announcements of planned unilateral reductions in Soviet forces, they have warned against overreacting to the proposed changes. Japanese commentaries on Gorbachev's December 1988 United Nations speech have cautioned that even if the proposed troop reductions affect Soviet forces stationed in the Far East, as now seems likely, the USSR could always remobilise and redeploy military forces there quickly so long as it maintains a military conscription system and weapons' stockpiles. They believe that Moscow may cut some obsolete vessels from the Pacific fleet, but it is unlikely to take steps that will lower the fleet's quality.[24]

So far, the changes made or announced in Soviet regional force deployments have not convinced Japanese officials to alter their own defence plans. Japan has continued a steady buildup of its own military forces and has taken steps to increase its security cooperation with the United States.

Soviet officials have criticised Japan's at best lukewarm reaction to Soviet regional arms control proposals and the continued increases in Japanese military expenditures and security cooperation with the United States. Most Soviet analysts do not perceive Japan as a threat by itself but they are concerned about the ways in which Japan's current and projected military deployment will increase the perceived US threat to Soviet interests in the Northwest Pacific. Currently, the Japanese are improving their surveillance capabilities so they can provide their own and US forces with real-time warning of Soviet naval and air movements to and from Soviet bases located around the Sea of Japan and the Sea of Okhotsk. Japanese forces are improving their mine-laying capabilities so they can bottle up the Soviet fleet in the Sea of Okhotsk and the Sea of Japan by mining the passageways between them and the Pacific. Japanese defence analysts perceive these improvements in their surveillance and mine-laying capa-

---

24. *Sankei,* January 31, 1989, p1 in *Daily Summary of the Japanese Press,* February 8, 1989, pp 8-9.

bilities as necessary if they are to fulfill their promised role of helping the United States to defend the sea lanes within a 1,000-mile radius of Japan. From the Soviet perspective, these Japanese measures would facilitate US efforts to attack Soviet Far East facilities and territory and Soviet strategic nuclear submarines deployed in the Sea of Okhotsk.

Soviet analysts are even more concerned about the military potential of Japan's enormous financial power and high technology capabilities. They were particularly disappointed by the failure of Soviet efforts to dissuade Japan from participating in Washington's strategic defence initiative research programme where it can make a contribution to the development of new, high technology weapons.

In sum, Gorbachev's territorial concessions so far have not gone far enough to meet Japanese demands. The continued territorial stalemate has acted as one obstacle to an expansion of Japanese trade and investment in the Soviet Union. Japanese security concerns have not been satisfied by recent unilateral changes in Soviet military deployments and activities. In reaction to the continued modernisation of Soviet Far East forces, Japan is building up its own military forces and increasing security cooperation with the United States in ways that Soviet policymakers perceive as threatening.

Prospects for change

In the short run, there is unlikely to be any radical change in Soviet-Japanese relations. Japan can be expected to continue its military buildup at a steady, but restrained pace. The current five-year medium-term defence plan governing the buildup of Japanese military forces expires at the end of fiscal 1990 (March 31, 1991). Japanese defence planners now are preparing the next five-year plan that will cover the period through the end of fiscal 1995.

While the details of the next defence plan will not be known until the summer of 1990, some aspects of it are being discussed in the Japanese press. According to press reports, the plan will be based on the 1976 Defence Plan General Outline which requires Japan to possess forces capable of repelling limited, small-scale aggression. Japan will continue to rely on the United States for nuclear deterrence and for assistance in repelling a large-scale conventional attack. Although the outline will not be revised, the attached table may be modified if it appears that the equipment listed in it will not allow Japan to fulfill its responsibilities of repelling small-scale aggression and providing for sealane defence.

The next defence plan will aim to correct deficiencies in Japan's current defence structure. It will set concrete goals for improvement in supplies, logistics, communications, intelligence, housing, research and development and the quality of military training.[25] To strengthen Japan's ground self-defence forces,

---

25.   *Sankei*, December 22, 1988, p2 in *Daily Summary of the Japanese Press*, December 30, 1988, pp 4-5; *Japan Economic Journal*, March 18, 1989, p15.

the plan will provide for the acquisition of a missile launcher system, long-distance surface-to-ship missiles and 10 squadrons of antitank helicopters.[26] Airborne warning and control systems (AWACs) will be acquired to improve Japanese capabilities to counter Soviet missile-bearing Backfire bombers and other planes which pose a threat to the sea lanes.[27] Interceptor units will be organised combining AWACs planes with F-15 fighters and mid-air refuelling planes.[28]

One can expect a continuing, steady buildup of Japanese military forces. However, there is little prospect in the near future, in the absence of a major crisis, that Japan will embark on a massive military buildup. Strong foreign opposition to a Japanese defence buildup and a lack of domestic support for any radical increase in Japanese defence spending[29] place clear limits on how much Japan will devote to defence. Japan will not return to the 1 per cent of Gross National Product limit on defence expenditures, adhered to between 1976 and 1986, but will observe the spirit of the 1 per cent limit by not allowing defence expenditures to greatly exceed it. Defence expenditures for the five years of the plan will be kept within an overall limit now expected to slightly exceed 20 trillion yen.[30] The continued buildup of Japan's military forces, even within these constraints, may make it more difficult for Soviet policymakers to win domestic support for significant reductions in their own Far East military deployments. However, Japanese public opinion and the JSP's coalition partners would prevent the JSP from radically altering Japan's security relationship with the United States. Both US and domestic pressure would militate against any radical reduction in Japanese defence spending.

Soviet-Japanese economic relations can be expected to expand at a moderate rate. Annual two-way trade, which is now approximately US$6 billion, is likely to increase at least marginally. The political pressure on Japan to reduce economic ties with the Republic of South Africa will encourage Japanese traders to increase the proportion of coal and rare metals such as platinum, imported from alternative suppliers including the USSR. The recent Soviet decision to import US$8 billion worth of consumer goods from Japan and other countries

26.   *Japan Economic Journal*, February 18, 1989, p15.

27.   Soviet Backfire bombers were deployed in naval and air aviation at around the same time which suggests that they have a sea interdiction role. Their range extends as far as the Philippines and they are capable of standoff launch of antiship missiles with a range of 500 miles. (Hisatomo Matsukane, 'Japan and security of the sea lanes,' Global Affairs, IV: 2 [Spring 1989], pp 49-64).

28.   *Yomiuri*, April 23, 1988, p1 in *Daily Summary of the Japanese Press*, May 18, 1989, pp 14-16.

29.   Two recent public opinion polls in mid-1988 and January 1989 indicate that between 77 and 79 per cent of Japanese favour either keeping the level of defence spending the same as now (48 per cent in one poll, 58 per cent in the other) or reducing it (31 per cent in one poll, 19.2 per cent in the other), (*Mainichi Daily News*, June 27, 1988, p1 and February 24, 1989, p1).

30.   *Japan Economic Journal*, March 18, 1989, p15. The annual average will not greatly exceed defence expenditures in fiscal year 1989 which have been set at 3.9198 trillion yen.

will have some positive impact on the level of Soviet-Japanese trade, particularly if the purchases are repeated in future years and if enough of the orders are directed toward Japan.[31]

Soviet-Japanese economic ties will be fostered by the proliferation of direct contacts between local authorities and enterprises in the Soviet Far East and East Siberia and Japanese trading firms, trading associations and regional and local governments. Large Japanese trading firms and trading associations representing medium and small Japanese firms are setting up offices in the Soviet Far East and sending trade missions there. One of these missions, a group of 130 high-powered executives from Japanese securities, life insurance, banking, trading and manufacturing firms visited Dalian and Harbin in China as well as Khabarovsk in the Soviet Far East to explore the possibilities for establishing trilateral projects. Japanese regional and local authorities in Niigata, Toyama, Kanagawa and Hokkaido are sending trade promotion missions to the USSR and organising trade promotion conferences. These conferences have involved participants from the Soviet Far East and from China's northeastern provinces which have become strong proponents of trilateral Sino-Soviet-Japanese trade. These burgeoning ties are being facilitated by the establishment of direct air and sea transportation links between Japan and the Soviet Far East.[32]

Multilateral joint ventures and trading arrangements are being considered that would involve Chinese, and in some cases North and South Korean partners as well as Soviet and Japanese firms. Some of the proposed arrangements would compensate for the absence of plentiful, cheap labour in the Soviet Far East and East Siberia by using Chinese or North Korean workers to produce goods for the Soviet market or to process Soviet timber and other raw materials for the Chinese or Soviet markets or for export to other countries.[33] For example, a private

---

31.   *Mainichi Daily News*, April 18, 1989, p5. Japan is not likely to be the cheapest source of supply for many of the desired light industrial products such as soap and detergent, razor blades, clothing, toothpaste, etc.

32.   *The Japan Economic Journal*, May 20, 1989, pp 2-3. A new triangular air route is being established linking Niigata, Harbin and Khabarovsk. Regular service on the Harbin-Khabarovsk leg is expected to begin in the summer of 1989. Chartered ferry and chartered air services are being established between Hokkaido and Sakhalin. In May 1989, a Soviet passenger liner sailed from Japan to Vladivostok carrying Japanese tourists and representatives from Niigata and Toyama prefectures.

33.   One such project is being promoted by Chung Joo-Young, honorary chairman and founder of the Hyundai group (Mainichi Daily News, February 3, 1989, p5), Ohta Seizo, president of Toho Mutual Life Insurance Company of Japan, has proposed a highly ambitious, multilateral joint venture that would involve Western and Japanese capital and technology, Soviet raw materials, Chinese and North Korean labour and South Korean production expertise in the development of 100 sq km of land in the town of Kraskino located near the Soviet borders with North Korea and China in a region rich in deposits of rare metals. Ohta envisages turning Kraskino into a major industrial centre through construction of a harbour, an airport and telecommunications facilities, and eventually factories, hotels and other facilities. (*The Japan Economic Journal*, December 24, 1988, p3). This region near the Soviet Union's borders with North Korea and China is being considered as one possible site for a special economic zone.

Japanese organisation, the Association for the Promotion of International Trade, is exploring the possibility of providing China with design and production equipment for the manufacture of textiles and consumer goods for the Soviet market. Japanese trading firms are acting as intermediaries in other Sino-Soviet trade arrangements. In a trilateral project begun in 1988, Tokyo Maruichi Shoji Company has been paying hard currency for the repair of Soviet fishing vessels in China and receiving in return Soviet refrigerated fish to market in Japan. Japanese trading firms hope to use their global sales networks to make other triangular arrangements that will get around the constraints imposed by Sino-Soviet barter trade.[34]

Even a slow, but steady expansion of Soviet-Japanese economic relations in the long run may have political effects. Soviet-Japanese economic relations are now dominated by large Japanese trading firms for whom Soviet trade is only an insignificant proportion of the total. For them, the pursuit of Soviet trade is not important enough to risk alienating hardline Foreign Ministry Soviet specialists intent on using trade as a lever with the USSR or the ire of US economic partners opposed to the sale of high technology to the Soviet Union.[35] If more medium and small size firms from Hokkaido and other relatively economically depressed regions of Japan become involved in trade and investment in the USSR, this could increase domestic support for better relations with the USSR.[36]

Resolution of the territorial dispute would also have a positive impact on Japanese attitudes toward the Soviet Union and on Soviet-Japanese economic relations. While there still are a number of serious obstacles to a territorial compromise, one should not be entirely ruled out given current signs of Soviet flexibility and Gorbachev's propensity for dramatic gestures. In return for a territorial compromise, Moscow undoubtedly would expect to receive large-scale Japanese governmental credits and support from Tokyo and from Japanese trading firms for the development of the Soviet Far East and East Siberia and for their economic integration into the Pacific community. However, a territorial compromise would mitigate, but not eliminate, Soviet-Japanese tensions arising from their opposing military deployments.

Medium and long term change

In the medium and long term, these tensions could be ameliorated by changes in the global and regional international environments, particularly in the state of Soviet-American relations. If Washington and Moscow conclude a strategic arms control agreement but fail to correct the conventional imbalance in Europe, this could increase American pressure on Japan to assume a larger share of the

34.   *The Japan Economic Journal*, May 20, 1989, pp 2-3.

35.   *The Mainichi Daily News*, December 19, 1988, p 12.

36.   This point was made in an unpublished paper by Professor Tsuyoshi Hasegawa of Hokkaido University's Slavic Research Centre.

common defence burden. If, on the other hand, as now seems more likely, there is successful conventional arms control in Europe and continued progress toward the resolution of regional conflicts in Southwest Asia, Indochina and on the Korean Peninsula, this would reduce the incentive for the United States to rely on the threat of offensive action in Northeast Asia as a deterrent to Soviet aggression elsewhere. A change of this kind would alter the rationale for US deployment of offensive forces and conduct of provocative military exercises in the region near Japan. It would make it more likely that Washington and Tokyo would support such regional confidence building measures as advance notification of and limitations on military exercises, exchanges of observers and on-site inspection. An improvement in Soviet-American relations also would have a positive impact on East-West trade although it would not end the restrictions on the sale of militarily useful high technology to the Soviet Union.

Besides these global factors, significant changes now taking place in the Asian international environment will have an important impact on Soviet-Japanese relations. Recently, there has been a decline in regional tensions and a marked proliferation of trade, sports, cultural and other exchanges between countries with strained or no diplomatic relations. A number of factors have produced these changes. One important change has been the growing desire of South Korea, Taiwan, and more recently, North Korea to guarantee their security by expanding the range of their international contacts. Another factor has been the efforts of the newly industrialising economies (NIEs) to find new markets as their exports face growing trade barriers in the United States and elsewhere. Still another impetus has come from the economic difficulties faced by the Asian socialist countries which have encouraged them to expand their economic ties with their capitalist neighbours. These changes have been facilitated by the improvement in Sino-Soviet relations which has facilitated progress toward the resolution of regional conflicts in Southwest Asia and in Indochina. The Sino-Soviet rapprochement has increased Vietnam's and Mongolia's diplomatic latitude and has encouraged Pyongyang to expand its range of diplomatic contacts because it no longer can count on making gains by playing China off against the Soviet Union. Hanoi's promise to withdraw its forces from Kampuchea has facilitated Soviet and Vietnamese efforts to improve relations with China and with non-communist Asian states.

The Soviet Union has taken advantage of these changes to expand its own economic ties with South Korea, Taiwan, the Philippines and other Asian capitalist countries. There have been parallel Japanese and in some cases US efforts to improve relations with Mongolia, Vietnam, North Korea and other Asian socialist countries and Chinese efforts to improve relations with India, Mongolia, Vietnam, Taiwan and Indonesia as well as with the USSR.

Whether or not Moscow will succeed in increasing economic integration with the Asia-Pacific region will depend in large measure on the success of Soviet economic and political reforms. If Soviet political and economic reform efforts fail and the USSR returns to its former policy of placing primary emphasis on the military, tensions between the Soviet Union and Japan and the Asia-Pacific countries could increase. If, on the other hand, Soviet economic and political reforms succeed and lead to increased Soviet economic, tourist, cultural, sports and other contacts with Japan and other non-socialist countries in the region, this will have a positive impact on the Asian international environment and on Soviet-Japanese relations.

This review has suggested that there is likely to be a slow, but steady improvement in Soviet-Japanese relations, reflecting changes in the global East-West and Asian regional environments. This scenario, however, presupposes the absence of a major Asian crisis and some continuity in the domestic political circumstances in the USSR. If a major crisis were to erupt on the Korean peninsula or elsewhere in Asia or if the Gorbachev leadership were to be replaced by a less reformist, nationalist alternative, the outcome could well be different.

Vietnam-China relations

BUI XUAN NINH
Senior Research Fellow, Institute for International Relations, Ministry of Foreign Affairs, Vietnam

CHINA, a big power with the largest population in the world, is wholly situated in the Asia-Pacific region. Due to its geo-political position, the centuries-old and close connection between China and this region is a natural one encompassing many fields — political, military, economic, cultural, ethnic and ethnological. History in the last decades shows that every development in the foreign policy of China has had immediate and direct, deep and profound impact on this region. It is our hope that China's modernisation programme will increase significantly its role in contributing, together with other major powers, to the cause of peace, stability and development in the Asia-Pacific region as a whole and particularly in Southeast Asia.

In the interest of world peace, one cannot but welcome the lessening of tensions and the improvement of relations between the big powers as in the case of the Soviet Union and the United States, and the normalisation of relations as in the case of China and the Soviet Union. These developments have created a sound political atmosphere and opened up a new era in international politics, especially in the Asia-Pacific. These developments clearly demonstrate also that with mutual understanding and constructive approaches from both sides, there is no obstacle, no conflict or dispute, no matter how big or complicated, that cannot be solved peacefully through direct dialogue and negotiation between the parties concerned if they are really determined to strive for peace and progress in the region as well as all over the world.

Being close neighbours, the Vietnamese value highly their traditional friendship with the Chinese. We will not relent in our efforts to achieve the normalisation of relations between the two countries. We firmly believe that whatever difficulties and complexities we still have to overcome, the present abnormal situation in the relations between China and Vietnam is only temporary. Despite ups and downs in the long history of the relations between Vietnam and China, the basic and traditional element is the aspiration for long term friendship between the two peoples. It is the right time to restore to our two peoples the opportunity to live in peace with each other.

Along with the settlement of the Kampuchean problem which is now at hand, two rounds of talks at the level of the deputy foreign ministers of Vietnam and China have been conducted in Peking since early 1989. We are hoping for the best and expect a positive and successful outcome. We are convinced that the restoration of friendly relations between Vietnam and China will be an important contribution to durable peace and security in the Asia-Pacific.

Relations among the big powers have undergone profound and rapid changes. As a member of the Southeast Asian community, we hope the new developments in big power relations will have positive impacts on the relations between Southeast Asia and the extra-regional major powers and on the relations between intra-regional countries. In today's world where economies are interrelated and linked, and where nations, large and small, developed or still developing, are interdependent, although each state has the growing capacity to affirm its independence, relations between states should be built along a new model.

As equal international entities, we should respect each other's independence and sovereignty and strictly abide by the lofty principles agreed upon by nearly 30 states at the historic Bandung Conference in 1955. We should respect the right of every people to choose their own way of life, to decide their own fate, and to resolve their own internal affairs. Non-intervention in one another's domestic affairs should be the norm of conduct among states, free from any kind of coercion (either political, economic or military), free from threat and use of violence.

Although national security is a legitimate concern of every state there should be equal security for all. Security of one state cannot be separated from that of other states. Especially, one cannot damage the security of others in the name of safeguarding one's own. The history of the world and of this region shows that conflicts between states threaten the security of all neighbouring countries and the region as a whole while the security of all is guaranteed by the security of each.

Ensuring peace and security in the region is not an easy task. Many problems remain — border disputes, contradictory territorial claims, and contradictions of interests resulting from social and economic development in individual countries. But for the sake of friendship, peace and stability, and in the real and long term national interest of each state, we should refrain from making the situation tense and dangerous and especially avoid resorting to acts of violence. If violence is allowed to be used, peace in the whole region will be immediately at stake. Maintaining the status quo, and conducting talks and negotiations with a spirit of realism and responsibility to peace and security of the region as a whole should be the right way to proceed before a legal agreement acceptable to all interested parties can be reached.

To further improve the friendly relations between states, problems involving third parties should not become obstacles to bilateral relations. At the same time bilateral relations should not be allowed to harm the interests of third parties. The encouragement and development of people diplomacy, of people-to-people dialogue and contact, and the exchange of friendly visits and cooperation between research institutions and educational, cultural and scientific organisations, will surely promote better understanding, friendship and prosperity.

As a neighbour, Vietnam earnestly hopes to live in peace and on good terms with China. Vietnam is also firmly set to improve its relations with other countries, first and foremost with the countries of this region. The Vietnamese people hope that relations between Vietnam and China, between China and other Southeast Asian countries, as well as relations between Vietnam and other countries in this region will develop further, soundly and effectively, in the interests of all, in conformity with the general trend we are witnessing in the world and in our region.

A step forward to peace on the Korean peninsula

RHEE SANG-WOO
*Professor of
Political Science,
Sogang University,
South Korea*

An overview

A NEW era of multilateral detente is dawning in Asia. The ideological barrier which had hindered the access of the non-socialist to the socialist nations has been lowered by Soviet and Chinese initiatives. Gorbachev's and Deng's policies of *glasnost* and *kaifeng* have been praised as signs of their intention to promote peaceful coexistence with non-socialist nations. The spirit underlying these open-door policies is a new paradigmatic idea of 'balance of interests' which has gradually replaced the old paradigm of 'balance of power'. The new thinking is based on the belief that the future international order will be sustained by a correlation of interests rather than military power. Even as the military destructive capability has become devastating, ironically military power has become useless as a means of diplomacy and can be likened to the saying that a long sword is not adequate to kill a mosquito. It is not difficult to imagine that in future a nation will comply more with another's demands when they share more interests in common than when it feels military threat from the other. The era of military power is ebbing. In East Asia a new regional order is emerging and a new complex cooperative system is being formulated.

Since last year, the government of the Republic of Korea (South Korea) under President Roh Tae Woo has been promoting its ambitious *realpolitik vis-a-vis* China and the Soviet Union. Putting politics aside for the moment, South Korea is trying to expand economic and cultural contacts with these two communist nations which are also North Korea's military allies and supporters in the hope that improved relations with them will reduce military tension on the Korean peninsula. Reactions of the two socialist neighbours have so far been positive and cooperative interactions are growing fast.

The new South Korean government has promulgated a new policy towards North Korea which was formally inaugurated in a July 7, 1988 declaration. The new policy is distinctively different from the previous one in its guiding philosophy, policy objectives and mode of policy implementation. Understanding that political unification through negotiation between the two Koreas which pursue diametrically opposing political ideals is not feasible at the moment, South Korea has decided to concentrate its initial effort on recovery of oneness of the 'Han (Korean) national community'. With the belief that 'politics is short, nation is eternal', the South Korean government has proposed, as an intermediate stage toward complete unification, a plan for a Han Commonwealth which is a socially, economically and culturally integrated community of the entire Korean people. It is felt that political integration will be much easier once there is societal unity.

North Korea, which has not yet shown any positive reaction to the South Korean initiative for inter-Korean detente, is still sticking to its hardline policy of ideological purity and refusing to formulate its own *perestroika* and *glasnost*. However, it is expected that eventually North Korea will realise that South Korea is sincere in promoting inter-Korean peace and North Korea will then make the appropriate response. Anyhow South Korea is prepared to implement all available measures to improve inter-Korean relations and take the initiative in promoting inter-Korean detente without waiting for North Korea's reciprocal actions out of a belief that good management of division will bring about earlier peace and unification.

Anatomy of the Korean problem

Two closely related but quite distinctive issues are involved in the 'Korean problem' — national reunification and institutionalisation of peace on the Korean peninsula. The national reunification goal is to restore unity of the Korean national community. It is a genuine intra-national issue which should be solved by the Koreans alone. The peace issue is however an international problem which is achievable only with the help of concerned neighbours. The two issues are closely inter-related. An agreement of peace between the two Koreas is a precondition of inter-Korean cooperation and without inter-Korean detente a regional peace system is unlikely to be worked out.

Ultimate goals of both North and South Korea are national reunification. North Korea wants to liberate South Korea's proletariat from 'exploitative class-enemies' and to install a unified socialist state throughout the entire Korean peninsula. On the other hand South Korea wants to establish a unified democratic Korea where all members of the Korean community, disregarding their class status, religion, property and beliefs are to enjoy equal rights and common prosperity. These two goals are logically incompatible and thus no compromise can be made through negotiation. Political reunification is to be postponed as a long-term objective of both Koreas until 'system compatibility' develops between the two Koreas through evolutionary changes of the current systems of the two Koreas.

If the ultimate goal of reunification is not achievable in the short term, then intermediate goals have to be considered. If we are to live in a divided Korea, we have to improve the divided situation. Beyond the political division line we have to develop non-political cooperative systems so that the people of the two Koreas are relieved from sufferings produced by the division. Divided families should be reunited, and social, cultural and economic interchanges should be promoted across the demilitarised zone (DMZ). Institutionalised peace should be worked out between the two Koreas so that people will no longer live under the threat of war. All of these tasks are to be contained in a concept of 'better management of division'.

If achievement of political unification is a long-term goal of the Korean people, management of division or promotion of constructive interchanges between the two Koreas is an intermediate goal and enhancement of inter-Korean peace is a most urgent short-term goal. Under the threat of war no interchanges are possible. Without increased interchanges between the two Koreas we cannot expect mutual trust to develop among the Koreans who have been separated for almost half a century. And yet without mutual trust no serious talks can be initiated for political unification. No matter how much time it will require we have to move forward step by step. No step can be skipped.

Inter-Korean peace

Institutionalising inter-Korean peace is an urgent task not only for the better management of the Korean division but also for regional peace in East Asia. To establish a new system of multilateral detente in Asia, the inter-Korean relationship, the only hostile one among all the bilateral relations within the region, should be improved.

How do we achieve peace between the two Koreas? First, the arms race should be halted. Then a safe and stable balance of forces should be installed. Finally a political agreement for peaceful resolution of the conflict should be worked out. If a system of international guarantee of peace is introduced, the peace system will be of a stabler form.

The core objective of inter-Korean arms control should be 'elimination of chances of outbreak of another full-scale war'. In order to achieve this objective, the war-fighting capabilities of both Koreas should be balanced. This means that neither side should have sufficient superiority of armed forces to override the other. Theoretically the control should first start by eliminating the disparity of forces through reducing the war-fighting capability of the superior side.

War-fighting ability consists of three basic elements: size of force, structure of forces, and deployment. Size of force is to be measured by the numbers, kinds and quality of the equipment or hardware. The number of soldiers is of secondary importance since these days armaments dominate the fighting ability. Of the total capabilities, the offensive elements of the forces have most significance in assessing military balance since it is with these elements that a nation can wage a war. Purely defensive forces do not harm peace much. The pattern of deployment is also an important element to be considered in the arms control for peace. Only offensively deployed forces menace the defenders in a *blitzkrieg*-type war.

At present North Korea has an edge over South Korea in all three dimensions of the military balance. Not only is the size of the North Korean armed forces bigger than South Korea's, but also North Korea's forces are designed for offensives. Furthermore, most of the offensive elements of the forces are deployed only 50km north of Seoul. Under these circumstances South Koreans are very much concerned with war deterrence. Inter-Korean relations, despite the political overtures for peaceful negotiations, are still volatile.

On confidence-building measures

At the moment both Koreas do not trust the other's intentions for peace. Mutual mistrust which developed from the past war experience still dominates the thinking of the two Koreas' leaders. In this situation no serious initiative for peace will develop from either side. To break the ice, some concrete measures to dispel mistrust should be worked out.

At this stage verbal pledges alone are not sufficient to convince the other side of the sincerity of any peace proposal. Visible actions are important. For example, if North Korea redeployed all of its offensive military units outside of the 200km perimeter of Seoul, South Korea will definitely honour North Korea's sincerity for arms control. If North Korea stops increasing the size of its offensive weapons, South Korea will definitely reconsider its plan for war deterrence. If North Korea accepts South Korea's proposal for on-site inspection of defence exercises, the atmosphere for arms limitation talks will be greatly improved.

I believe that North Korean military experts understand South Korea's armed forces are not offensive-oriented. For example South Korea has only 1,500 tanks compared to North Korea's 3,500 and only two of South Korea's infantry divisions are mechanised while North Korea has one motorised infantry division and 23 mechanised brigades. In the air, too, South Korea does not have any bomber while North Korea has 83. The South Korean air force consists of only interceptors and fighters for air defence. If North Korea transforms its force structure into a defensive one like South Korea's, it will help South Koreans believe in North Korea's pledge of non-aggression.

Besides direct military measures, promotion of non-political interaction between the two Koreas will definitely enhance mutual trust. Both Koreas once

Military balance of South and North Korea

	North Korea	South Korea
Armed personnel	1,000,000	650,000
Ground forces		
infantry division	30	21
mechanised division	-	2
armoured division	1	-
motorised division	1	-
reserves division	29	25
infantry brigade	4	
mechanised brigade	23	15
armoured brigade	12	
special combat brigade	22	
tanks	3,500	1,500
AFV	1,960	1,550
Naval forces		
submarine	23	3
destroyer/sub-chaser	32	29
missile gunboats	30	11
patrol boats	106	94
torpedo boats	173	-
landing ship	126	52
Air forces		
bombers	83	-
ground attackers	30	23
fighters	907	457
support aircraft	780	690

Source:
Chung Byung-Ho, *Nambukhan Kunsaryok, 1989*

agreed to develop various exchange programmes including family reunion, economic exchange and cultural cooperation but talks for the promotion of these programmes have been suspended. Resumption of these talks will contribute to enhancing the mutual confidence necessary for the initiation of peace talks between the two Koreas.

Conclusion

Asians are now working hard to bring about a new regional peace system based on multilateral detente. Thanks to Chinese and Soviet initiatives for lowering ideological barriers through their new policies of *kaifeng* and *glasnost*, an era of peace is at hand. We Koreans in North and South Korea alike are obliged to cooperate in peace-fostering efforts of our Asian neighbours. South Korea has discarded its previous policy of endless competition with North Korea and has adopted a new policy of detente with North Korea and other socialist neighbours extending beyond the ideological barriers. South Korea is removing the wall built by itself between the two Koreas, thus leaving only the wall built by its North Korean brethren. If North Korea responds to the South Korean initiative, then inter-Korean peace can be realised.

A realistic approach should be adopted in the resolution of the age-old inter-Korean conflict. Leaving our dream of a fully united Korea to the future, we should start to work out concrete measures for better management of division. We should install peace between the two parts of Korea first and work out ways to reduce the suffering of people which has resulted from the hostile competition between the two Koreas. We should also try to maintain the oneness of the Korean national unity through increased exchanges between the divided parts so that someday we can pursue political integration. While we maintain 'we-feelings' among all Koreans we shall be united anyway. To reiterate, let us not forget that 'politics is short, nation is eternal'.

The Korean conflict in the short, medium and long term

RYO SUNG CHOL
*Deputy Director,
Institute for
Disarmament and
Peace, North Korea*

KOREA, situated at a strategic position in Northeast Asia, is a country rich in natural resources with almost all chemical elements. For these reasons, the big powers have scrambled to seize the country's strategic and economic resources from as far back as when Korea entered contemporary history. The competition of the big powers over the Korean peninsula has left irrevocable after-effects on the development of the peninsula's modern history. Their scrambles at the close of the 19th century converted Korea into a colony of Japanese imperialists and the imperialist powers' confrontation under the pretext of checking communism in the 1940s partitioned Korea into two and created the Korean question, an issue of concern in the international community.

The Korean people have to date faced the tragedy of national division for 40 years. Korea's division is not the result of the development of its internal situation, much less of the will of the Korean people. Because of the demands of US policy which included in its responsible zone the ancient city of Seoul and Inchon, a port of strategic importance during the Pacific war, latitude 38 degrees North became a military boundary line. This line was also fixed as a political boundary splitting the Korean nation itself beyond the military sense because the United States did not implement the decision of the Moscow Three Foreign Ministers' Conference but conducted a separate election in South Korea.

The division of Korea after its liberation from the Japanese contravenes the purpose of war of the Allied nations in World War II and is an unlawful act which cannot be justified by any reason. The Korean peninsula has been fraught with discord and tension because this division has turned into a worldwide confrontation point between two social systems and two ideas under the constant interference and influence of foreign forces. The 250 km-long Military Demarcation Line across the Korean peninsula has been reinforced with a seven-metre high concrete wall and wire entanglements, and turned into a roadblock where communications between separated relatives are banned.

Developments on the Korean peninsula over the last 40 years have been characterised by foreign interference, national division and the consequent aggravation of tension. Therefore, the essense of the Korean question today is: firstly, a matter of excluding the interference of foreign forces and regaining the national sovereignty of the Korean people; secondly, a matter of reunifying a nation and a country which were separated temporarily; and thirdly, a matter of eliminating the root cause of war and tension in Asia.

Proceeding from this essence of the Korean question, we maintain the principle that Korea's reunification should be achieved independently without interference by foreign forces, by peaceful means through contacts and dialogues without resorting to armed forces, and through national unity transcending differing ideas and social systems. These three principles of independence, peace and national unity are the principles of national reunification which were confirmed jointly by North and South Korea before the whole nation through the July 4 North-South Joint Statement in 1972 which was officially recognised by the world. North and South, however, still fail to agree on detailed ways of reunifying the divided country.

Today a global process of dialogue and reconciliation is rapidly developing and many regional disputes which exerted a negative influence on peace and security are being settled favourably. The Korean question remains the last legacy of the cold war and an outstanding issue whose solution brooks no further delay. With a view to solving the Korean question, the circumstances for the Korean people themselves to determine their problem independently must be created.

Korea was partitioned by outside forces. That is why the process for reunification must inevitably be accompanied by the process of removing the influence of foreign forces. This requirement is expressly stipulated in the term 'independence' in the first of the three principles of national reunification recognised by North and South Korea and the international community. In a joint document on the Korean issue announced in Almaata in August 1988, Soviet and American scholars also recognised and emphasised that the question of Korea's reunification is an internal issue of the Korean people.

Legal and practical steps should be taken so that the Korean people, the masters of the Korean issue, can settle the reunification question in accordance with their own judgement and decision without any foreign interference. Here a rather heavy responsibility rests with the US which has stationed armed forces in South Korea, controls the operational command of the South Korean army and has a historical involvement in the Korean question. The United States, which participated in the Moscow Three Foreign Ministers' Conference, is duty-bound to leave the Korean people to decide their destiny by themselves.

What is important also for the settlement of the Korean question is to agree upon the most reasonable way of national reunification. The process of reunifying the divided country is the process of unifying the territory, population and the power organ, the three bases of the existence of a state. The main thing here is to determine how to unify the legislative and administrative structures of the two regions exercising their respective jurisdictions.

To solve this matter, we cannot but take into consideration the following specific conditions of Korea:

- Firstly, the present-day fixed reality of Korea in which different ideas and social systems have existed in North and South for 40 years;
- Secondly, the present aspirations of the Korean people to reunify the country on the principle of co-existence in which one side recognises and tolerates the other side, neither conquering nor overwhelming the other side.

In the final analysis, we have reached the practical conclusion that confederation is the most reasonable and realistic way of national reunification.

To those who would question whether an unprecedented confederation is feasible between two regions with no community in ideas and social systems, I would like to suggest here some positive answers:

- Different economic forms may exist in a country and accordingly a superstructure commensurate with such economic forms — namely different ideas, ideals and ethics — may exist.
- An absolute majority agree that a reunification related to the destiny of the whole nation holds priority for the social system related to the interests of the individual classes and sections.

Therefore, we consider that the objections of some sections within both social systems over the mode of social embodiment cannot constitute an absolute factor for impeding the reunification and prosperity of the whole nation.

Proceeding from the specific conditions prevailing in Korea, we think that in order to establish a unified state structure on the Korean peninsula at present, there is no other practical way to ensure legality than through a confederation method. A confederal republic will internally base its policy on democracy, a common political idea which can be approved and accepted by anyone, and hold fast to the non-aligned and neutral line externally. Democracy and neutrality are common denominators which can be accepted by both sides without objection since the two different social systems form a confederation. Democracy and neutrality are also fair means stipulating that no one side can impose its ideas and social system on the other.

If this kind of confederal state is established on the Korean peninsula, it will protect the foreign economic concessions already invested there. The establishment and prosperity of a democractic and neutral confederal state on the Korean peninsula will conform to the national aspirations of the Korean people as well as the purposes of the Cairo Declaration of 1943 and the Decisions of the Moscow Three Foreign Ministers' Conference of 1945 and benefit peace, security and cooperation in the Asia-Pacific region.

For the settlement of the Korean question it is imperative to relax tension and guarantee peace on the Korean peninsula. At present, the density of military forces and equipment and deployment of nuclear weapons on the Korean peninsula has reached a higher degree than in any other region in the world and the danger of armed conflict is increasing daily. Without converting this unstable state into a durable peace on the Korean peninsula, we cannot talk about the peaceful reunification of Korea and the security of the Asia-Pacific region.

In order to ease tension and guarantee peace on the Korean peninsula, it is imperative, firstly, to ensure legal guarantees for advancing beyond the present state of ceasefire and ensure a durable peace, and secondly, to drastically reduce the armed forces in North and South Korea and eliminate each other's attack capability.

With a view to proceeding beyond the current abnormal situation on the Korean peninsula where an unstable semi-war state has lasted for nearly 40 years, the conclusion of a peace agreement replacing the armistice agreement in accordance with the preceding practices between belligerents is an unavoidable task whose solution brooks no further delay — not only for the Korean people's cause of reunification but also for peace in Asia and the world at large.

The current Korean Armistice Agreement was signed between the Korean and Chinese armies on one side and the United Nations forces on the other side. The responsibility for the implementation of the Armistice Agreement in Korea rests with the Korean People's Army in the north and with the US forces in the south. The United States is the only country which has stationed armed forces on the Korean peninsula and it seizes even the operational prerogative of the South Korean army. For this reason, the question of replacing the Korean Armistice Agreement must be considered by North Korea and the United States and a peace agreement concluded also between them.

In international law, a country which 'contributed' its army to the United Nations cannot be a neutral state in the relevant war. The United States was not a neutral state but a belligerent one in the Korean war. Therefore, we believe that the United States' participation in the legal acts to replace the Korean Armistice Agreement with a peace agreement is extremely reasonable either in view of its responsibility for the Korean question or in the light of its commitment to peace before the world people, and that its action would be a good yardstick of its sincerity.

At the same time, North and South Korea must pledge before the whole nation and the international community not to attack each other, so as to create a peaceful environment for national reunification. A durable peace will be maintained on the Korean peninsula when legal guarantees such as the conclusion of a peace agreement between North Korea and the United States and the adoption of a declaration of non-aggression between North and South Korea are given.

Next, we consider it necessary and inevitable to cut drastically the armed forces and eliminate the attack capability of both sides in order to liquidate the factors which may trigger off a new war on the Korean peninsula. Today in Korea huge armed forces are sharply confronted with the Military Demarcation Line in between and a dangerous situation persists in which a war may break out at any moment owing to an accidental event. Therefore, in 1988 North Korea advanced a disarmament proposal on reducing the armed forces of North and South by withdrawing the US troops in three phases by the end of 1991 and thus maintaining the armed forces of both sides at less than 100,000-strong from 1992. When this proposal is carried into effect, the Korean peninsula will be converted into a nuclear-free, peace zone without the danger of military confrontation.

We consider this proposal to be the best confidence-building measure to guarantee peace and solve the question of reunification on the Korean peninsula. We envisage introducing a fair verification system in trimming the armed forces of North and South. We propose to inform the other side of the progress of each other's military reduction and make them public, and increase the authority of the Neutral Nations Supervisory Commission in Panmunjom to verify and confirm the progress. We also deem it necessary and reasonable to set up a neutral zone in the contact line of both sides and deploy a neutral nations inspection force in order to guarantee peace during and after the period of arms reduction.

Under the circumstances in which nuclear disarmament has been started between the Soviet Union and the United States, with the Soviet Far East forces reduced and the Chinese armed forces drastically cut down, there is no ground whatsoever for our counterpart not to accept our detente proposal in which we showed our goodwill in unilaterally cutting our military forces to 100,000.

We consider these fair proposals to rationally settle the Korean question at the earliest possible date without infringing upon the interests of either the United States or South Korea.

We do not deny that the opposite side also has its own views and apprehension. The best way to solve them is through dialogue and negotiation. In order to ease the present tension and guarantee peace in Korea, it is necessary first of all to hold tripartite talks between North and South Korea and the United States. To get North and South Korea, the parties directly concerned in the Korean question, and the United States to sit together is the most idealistic and reasonable way towards guaranteeing peace on the Korean peninsula. Tripartite talks can be a form of negotiation too should they be initiated and requested by the United States. During such talks, the Korean question can be discussed as well as the improvement of North Korea-US relations. However, the United States may have bilateral talks with us at present if it deems it inconvenient to hold tripartite talks.

Next, for the settlement of the reunification question, multi-channelled dialogues and contacts should be arranged between North and South Korea. Today an important matter for the solution of national reunification is to determine a reasonable way of reunification. To this end, it is imperative to hold a political consultative meeting of leadership-level people of North and South Korea.

Since the reunification question is a matter related to the destiny of the whole nation as well as the interests of all groupings and strata, it can be solved only by mobilising the will of the whole nation. Therefore, this matter must be discussed in a broad-based political consultative conference representing political parties, social organisations and groupings of all strata. However, since this kind of consultative meeting is impossible at this moment, the best way of collecting the views of the entire nation and discussing and confirming the reunification question is to get leadership-level people including the authorities who can represent people of all strata to sit together.

The reunification debate is not a matter that only the authorities could monopolise and manage. A government should not deprive the masses of the right to speak about such national issues like reunification. An important way of settling the reunification question is to develop multi-channelled contacts and dialogues including high-level talks to ease tension, remove political and military confrontation and effect interchanges and cooperation between North and South.

Our proposed negotiation should involve all the matters to be solved between the two sides, from political to humanitarian issues, and the negotiating parties should include representatives from all strata, from president to students. Our patriotic proposals, however, are challenged by the Team Spirit joint military exercises, by the imprisonment and punishment of those who came to Pyongyang to discuss reunification with us on charges of espionage, and of those people who demand independence, democracy and reunification on charges of being 'leftist pro-communist forces'.

We hope that the South Korean authorities would not complicate the situation but return to a sincere stance to achieve peace and peaceful reunification on the Korean peninsula and encourage and promote multi-channelled contacts and dialogue between North and South.

The Korean people will observe the 50th anniversary of national liberation in 1995. North Korea appealed some time ago to its fellow countrymen to make 1995 a historic year of national peaceful reunification. I hope that all the scholars present here will pool their wisdom and efforts to help the Korean people in their struggle to ensure peace and achieve reunification on the Korean peninsula.

The Cambodian conflict, 1978-1989

MOHAMED NOORDIN SOPIEE
Director-General, Institute of Strategic and International Studies (ISIS) Malaysia

Introduction

About endgames

AS every chess theoretician knows, there are three parts in every game. There is the opening, the middle game, and the endgame. The Cambodian endgame is one and a half years old. Although there is likely to be a resumption of another game of conflict at the end of the present one, it is probable that the Cambodian conflict that began with the Vietnamese invasion of December 1978 will end before the end of 1989. The new game will not be quite the same.

As every good chess theoretician ought to know, there are four outcomes of the endgame. Regardless of his position and that of his opponent, the beginner merely attempts a win or may concede defeat. The more tutored may at some point manoeuvre for a draw. The fourth option is to abandon the game.

Even at this stage, and in mid-1989, it is useful to make the point that with regard to Indochina, there was a messy settlement of the Vietnam conflict in 1954 and again in 1973; there was a messy settlement in the case of Laos in 1962 and then again in 1974. The future 'settlement' of the Cambodian conflict could be relatively 'clean' or quite 'messy'. At this stage, it is important not to give up on the struggle for a comprehensive political settlement. At the same time, it is crucial to consider the reality that the 'best' may be an enemy of the 'acceptable'. And the choice we have before us is not between the 'good' and the 'bad' but between the 'bad' and the 'problematical' and the 'worse' and the 'even more problematical'.

About the players

Without in any way minimising the centrality of the Vietnamese military invasion, it is analytically important to recognise that the Cambodian conflict is both an internal as well as an international conflict. There are politically four players (for now) to the internal conflict: the Khmer Rouge, the KPNLF (Khmer People's National Liberation Front), the Sihanoukists (in a loose Coalition Government of Democratic Kampuchea [CGDK] legally recognised by the United Nations) and the regime under Hun Sen (fully supported and backed by the Vietnamese).

At the international level, on one side is the People's Republic of China (PRC), Thailand and the Asean states and the United States (and others). On the other side is Vietnam and the Soviet Union (and others).

I.　Positive factors affecting prospects for a resolution

The momentum towards a negotiated settlement

For almost exactly nine years, the Cambodian conflict was stuck in a stalemated middle game. The stalemate served the interests of China, the United States, Thailand and the Asean states as a group. The Soviet Union, Vietnam and the Khmer people were the primary sufferers, in that ascending order of severity. They have been caught in a 'trap' from which they could not extricate themselves.

Then, Prince Sihanouk moved, to the consternation of both China and Thailand. In January 1988, Prince Sihanouk and Hun Sen met for a second time in Paris. Indonesia then took the initiative to convene the Jakarta Informal Meeting (JIM) which met in July 1988.

In June, the 12th round of Sino-Soviet normalisation talks was convened in Moscow. This was followed by the first high-level discussions on Cambodia between the PRC and the USSR in Beijing in August. The first meeting of the JIM Working Group met in October. In November, Prince Sihanouk, Son Sann and Hun Sen met in Paris. In December Chinese Foreign Minister Qian Qichen went to Moscow. And before the end of the year, Siddhi Savetsila, who is not well known for being either naive or soft-headed, had given it as his opinion that 'We have almost reached the end of the tunnel. We can see the light'.

1989 has seen a speed-up of the momentum. On January 9-12 the Foreign Ministers of Thailand and Vietnam met in Hanoi. On January 16-18 Vietnamese First Deputy Foreign Minister Dinh Nho Liem and Chinese Vice-Minister Liu Shuqing met in a pathbreaking meeting in Beijing. In a surprise (to 'shocking') move, Hun Sen was invited by and met Thai Premier Chatichai Choonhavan in Bangkok. Foreign Minister Siddhi Savetsila flew off to Beijing for a meeting with his Chinese counterpart. The three Khmer resistance factions met for the first time in 18 months in the Chinese capital to map out their strategy for JIM II, which was held, with somewhat disappointing results, from February 19-21 in Jakarta. The flurry of activity has continued to the present time. (The momentum of meetings can be expected to persist despite dead-end, deadlock and disappointment).

The next important dates on the schedule are July 24 when Prince Sihanouk and Hun Sen will be meeting again, July 25 when all the Cambodian parties are scheduled to meet, and August 1989 when the first meeting of the International Conference intended to set up an International Control Commission will be convened in Paris.

Agreement on previous points of contention

Amidst the to-ing and fro-ing, the Khmer Rouge has been forced to come forth with proposals of its own; it is now clear to everyone that the Soviet Union wants to settle quickly; Vietnam has in fact withdrawn a very large number of troops from Cambodia and convinced just about everyone (including all the three factions in the CGDK) that it is serious about total troop withdrawal by September 30, 1989 under almost all likely conditions.

Everyone is now agreed (in public at least) that the completion of total Vietnamese troop withdrawal should also see the complete termination of all foreign military assistance to all factions in conflict in Cambodia (despite previous Thai and Chinese opposition to linking Vietnamese withdrawal to anything).

All, including the Khmer Rouge, are agreed that machinery and forces must be in place to prevent 'a return to genocidal policies'. And that conditions must be created to prevent the Khmer Rouge from returning to exclusive power in the future. China now goes along fully with this. Indeed, at the February 9 meeting of the three factions of the CGDK held in Beijing, the Khmer Rouge was party to the joint statement calling for a 2,000-strong UN supervisory force that would not only keep Vietnam out of Cambodia but also 'block a return to power by the Khmer Rouge'.

Despite the Hun Sen regime's and Vietnam's emotional preference for the contrary, all parties are agreed that the Khmer Rouge should be encouraged to take part in an internal political settlement and in the national reconciliation process. (If they do not do so peacefully, they will simply do so by other means). As part of this process also, it is agreed (at least in declaratory terms) that all parties should be allowed to take part in general elections and that some form of multipartite body should be established to determine how elections to a representative national assembly should proceed.

There is also full agreement on the introduction of some international mechanism and on an international conference on Cambodia (due to meet in Paris in August).

It should be noted that with regard to many of these areas of agreement, there is a multitude of disagreement on many nuts and bolts. There is a lot of the devil in the details. Agreements in principle can be another thing when one goes from the abstract to the concrete. There are enormous possibilities for disagreeing later on with regard to what has been previously agreed to. Having said all this, it is equally clear that there has most certainly been great movement.

At the last Asia-Pacific Roundtable a year ago, my paper on 'Kampuchea: One Way Forward' dwelt at some length on the various possible solutions for Cambodia —10 to be exact — suggesting that Thailand would settle for a continuation of the stalemate whilst wishing for a pro-Thailand Cambodia (referred to as the 'Austrian Solution'). It was suggested that China at that stage still preferred a pro-Beijing Cambodia dominated by a moderated Khmer Rouge (referred to as the 'Democratic Kampuchea Solution') although it was fully committed to a maintenance of the stalemate as the first best practical option. It was also suggested that at that stage Vietnam's preference was for the 'Laos Solution', for a Cambodia that would be legally sovereign but less than politically independent, a Cambodia that would not threaten Thailand but one that would take into the fullest account the interests and policies of Vietnam on all the major issues, that unswervingly has to go along with Hanoi on all the critical issues and that has a powerful Vietnamese military presence.

It was then suggested that a possible compromise solution (defined as 'Solution Five') would be a territorially intact Cambodia that is:

- Legally sovereign,
- Fully independent,
- Regionally neutral but sensitive to its neighbours,
- Internationally non-aligned, and
- Generally peaceful (but with continuing internal threats to peace)
- Reasonably politically stable, and
- Unthreatening to both Vietnam and Thailand.

Whatever their maximalist preferences, it would appear that as of today all the critical players (including the Khmer Rouge) and the supporting cast find nothing objectionable to such a solution. It is now acceptable to all.

The distance that has been travelled with regard to the end state is not a short one. The real-world problem now is how to get from here to there.

There are of course two conditions for a speedy resolution of any conflict. First, the critical actors must want a speedy resolution. Second, they must be able to work out the essential terms for a viable solution (which is very often closely connected with just how badly they want such a solution).

On this score, there is much good news to report with regard to the external actors to the Cambodian conflict. Besides the 'settlement momentum' and agreement today on many important points of previous contention, the present policies of the Soviet Union, Vietnam, Thailand and China constitute the third positive factor working for a speedy solution of the Cambodian conflict.

Present policies of the USSR, Vietnam, Thailand and China

USSR policy. There are those who believe that the Soviet Union is a recent convert to a speedy resolution of the Cambodian conflict. That view is erroneous. Indeed, the Soviet Union was the first external party to be committed to a quick solution (provided of course that it was one that did not sacrifice its alliance with Vietnam or its facilities in that country).

Even before Gorbachev, the Soviet Union had seen much virtue in a speedy resolution. The reasons were and are obvious.

First and foremost, continuation of the Cambodian problem was a most serious obstacle to Moscow's rapprochement with China. Second, it opened the way for PRC advancement in the Pacific, particularly in the Asean community, and most dramatically with regard to Thailand. Third, it was a great help to the United States diplomatically and politically amongst the same set of states. Fourth, it was an obstacle to political, diplomatic and economic Soviet advance in the region. Fifth, especially in the Gorbachev years, being on the less favoured side at the UN and globally was not particularly helpful in creating a new image of the Soviet Union worldwide.

The Soviet Union believed then as it believes now that its position *vis-a-vis* Vietnam and Indochina can be secured without the Cambodian albatross around its neck, provided of course that no serious offence was caused to Vietnam. Most clearly, Gorbachev's Soviet Union has exerted the most substantial pressure on the Vietnamese to pull out their troops and to be flexible on the entire Cambodian question.

Vietnamese policy. Whilst there appears to be some dissent in Vietnam about unilaterally and unconditionally pulling out all Vietnamese troops from Cambodia by the end of September and about 'Solution Five' (analogous to the position of Finland today) in general, there seems little doubt now that the present Vietnamese leadership is indeed committed to a total withdrawal under most conditions and is willing to accept Solution Five. The reasons for this are equally clear.

Vietnam today faces many domestic pressures and troubles. Its economy is under the most serious strain. More than 10 years of military effort and unrealistic expectations on what it would take to do what it had to do in Cambodia have made the Vietnamese people and most of their leaders weary of the war. Hanoi has revealed that in all, its conflict with Cambodia has cost it 60,000 casualties. Politically, therefore, there is a need to bring the boys home.

Financially, there is need to reduce the burdens of occupation and to secure much needed foreign aid and loans. (A reported US$2 billion a year from the USSR is not enough quantitatively and qualitatively). The financial burdens are heavy. The cost in terms of opportunity costs is great.

Strategically, there is a need to make peace with a PRC which has indeed bled Vietnam white, and to concede to Soviet pressure.

Diplomatically, the sense of diplomatic isolation, which is supposed to leave men of steel completely unmoved, has had its bite.

Economically, the demands of its own *perestroika* are seen to dictate an opening to the world, to foreign investment, foreign technology and foreign trade, things not possible for so long as it remains militarily in Cambodia.

Emotionally, the force of Vietnamese nationalism makes over-dependence on the Soviet Union a most uncomfortable position.

Psychologically, the Vietnamese who cannot but see the undeniable and dramatic economic advancement of their neighbours in Asean are unprepared to see their country fall backward into time, squeezed between an expected Chinese economic giant and a dramatically growing Thailand/Asean.

The other two critical external players in the Cambodian game are of course Thailand and China, both of which were until recent months unyielding in their commitment to a continued stalemate.

Thai policy. The Thai turnaround is testimony to the difference that the leadership of Chatichai Choonhavan has made. To be sure, there are now two and a half official Cambodia policies coming out of Bangkok. The Chatichai line has not overwhelmed the others. But it is a dramatic change which takes Thailand out as the hardliner of Asean.But the explanation has to go beyond personality.

Underlying it is the supreme sense of confidence now existing in Bangkok, a supreme confidence founded on a realistic assessment of the Vietnamese threat and Thailand's dramatic economic performance especially in the last two years. The force of Thai capitalist dynamism and expansionism has to be reckoned with. Mixed with this heady brew are expectations about the economic potential of Vietnam, Cambodia and Laos. Whereas before Thailand was a frontline state under threat of attack, it is now a frontline state ready to advance.

PRC policy. The equally unexpected changes in Beijing have been as important. The extent of change must not be exaggerated. There are those who argue that the change in the PRC policy was purely tactical, that the Chinese cannot and will not be prepared to abandon the Khmer Rouge. (The relatively kind words at the time of the first high-level meeting in 10 years between Vietnam's First Deputy Foreign Minister Dinh Nho Liem and Chinese Vice-Minister Liu Shuqing [January 16-18] should be compared with the views expressed by Chinese Foreign Minister Qian Qichen in an interview with *The New York Times* on February 21, the eve of George Bush's visit to China and at the end of the JIM II meeting in Bogor. In discussing Cambodia, Qian strongly criticised Vietnam and said: 'Vietnam is not trustworthy. We cannot believe its words, and the international community should exert more pressure on it'). The Second China-Vietnam Vice-Ministerial Meeting was also barren of even declaratory result. The impact of Tiananmen is not known. But it would be surprising if the Chinese do not continue to be under pressure for a settlement of the Cambodian problem and if they revert to their commitment to a protracted stalemate — their position in the middle game.

For the moment, the Chinese may not quite have their heart in it. But there is little doubt about where their minds have told them to go.

If China does not today stand for movement towards a negotiated settlement, it will increasingly stand alone, a prospect that it may now find even less attractive. In any case, the lesson has been taught, the objectives have been won. Vietnam has been bled. The Vietnamese have withdrawn troops (50,000 in 1988) and seem intent on total troop withdrawal by a self-set September 1989 deadline. Hanoi has consciously and deliberately gone through the process of atonement. With the Thai turnaround, there is no longer the necessity to demonstrate inflexibility.

Nayan Chanda has argued that Peking also seems to have reached the conclusion 'that it has reached the limit of what it can achieve in Cambodia through its Khmer Rouge allies whose inability to defeat the Vietnamese and whose blood-stained image makes them a diminishing asset.' Like every other civilised nation, and after Tiananmen, China may want even less to be seen huddled around the same campfire with the Khmer Rouge. Perhaps there has for some time been no great need to ensure a very pro-China Cambodia since Beijing has secured a firm friend in a dynamic Thailand, and there is little prospect in the foreseeable future of a consolidated Indochina under an antagonistic and strong Hanoi.

It is even possible that what the Chinese used to state as the most serious obstacle to closer relations with the USSR may become an obstacle to the Chinese getting closer to the Soviet Union, in a situation where there is a more equal desire for much better relations — even with an increasingly besieged Gorbachev Soviet Union.

Other positive factors working for reconciliation at the international level

Clearly a most positive, additional factor also working for an early resolution of the Cambodian conflict is the weariness that all the critical players seem to feel with regard to the present stalemate. All the external players appear 'tired' of 'Cambodia'.

There are other positive factors working at the *international level*. Not the least of these is the desire to turn even further inward towards great domestic missions and preoccupations on the part of the external communist players: the USSR, China and Vietnam.

Other big positive developments have been:

(1) The momentum of Sino-Soviet rapprochement, which has truly picked up steam,
(2) The movement towards regional reconciliation between Thailand and Vietnam,
(3) The beginning of a (difficult) thaw in the relations between China and Vietnam,
(4) The 'promising' start to establishing good relations between Bangkok and Vientiane, and
(5) The start of a Thai *modus vivendi* with Hun Sen's Phnom Penh.

These five rapprochements have come within an incredibly short space of time and are extremely positive developments (not only with regard to the Cambodian conflict of course).

All these have led to somewhat new atmospherics, whose positive feedback effect in creating the ambience for further reconciliation as well as cooperation should not be underestimated.

Compared to this array of positive fundamentals working for reconciliation at the international level of the Cambodian conflict, it is difficult to marshall a list of factors working in the other direction.

This unfortunately cannot be said with regard to the *internal dimensions*, although it is important to recognise that there indeed are positive factors working for Khmer national reconciliation.

Factors working for Khmer national reconciliation

Whatever is said about any of the present four Cambodian factions, there is no denying the force of Khmer nationalism. All four factions are at this stage deeply concerned about the survival of the Cambodian state. After all, the largest concentrations of Khmers today are firstly in Phnom Penh, secondly on the Thai side of the Cambodian border and thirdly, in Orange Country, California. There are indeed good reasons to worry about whether much further delay will not destroy the fundamental hardware, software and peopleware needed for the existence of an independent state of Cambodia.

Second, there would appear to be 'killing fatigue' and 'fighting fatigue' on all sides, not at all surprising when it is remembered that from the time of the Sihanouk overthrow to the Khmer Rouge takeover in 1975, possibly as many as 600,000 people died. The killings of the Khmer Rouge period are too distressful to elaborate. The last 10 years have seen, comparatively, very few killings. But the dying did not end in 1978 and half a million Khmers are today refugees. The principle problem is that many of the Khmer Rouge leaders have not had enough and will still be interested in carrying on the military path to power.

Third, although the Hun Sen regime has made tremendous strides in establishing their *de facto* administration in Cambodia, there is the widespread realisation amongst them that they cannot achieve total dominance and ensure the absence of fighting conducted by the Khmer Rouge and the non-communist resistance in the shorter term; and there is realisation on the side of the resistance (including the Khmer Rouge) that they cannot now and in the near future destroy or displace the Hun Sen regime.

Fourth, all the Khmer factions cannot ignore the changing international environment and the pressures arising from the present policies of their backers. Unfortunately, however, the Cambodian conflict is not a proxy war and not for the first time are we seeing instances of the supposed tail wagging the supposed head.

II. Negative factors working against national reconciliation

Unfortunately, however forceful some of the above realities are, there are for the moment stronger factors working against national reconciliation. The sense of mutual suspicion, mutual contempt and often mutual hatred is understandably intense. (In June in Beijing, for example, Prince Sihanouk said: 'One has either to be naive or an idiot to believe that the Khmer Rouge of the 1980s can be different from the Khmer Rouge of the 1970s').

Secondly, there is the problem of unequal strengths on the ground, in reality. Yet according to the formula put forward by the CGDK, there is to be an equal, quadripartite government. Such a government, should it be possible, can only come about through compromise. It would mean an unequal burden of sacrifice and an unequal boon of benefit. The Hun Sen regime believes that it is in control of most of Cambodia. Why should it give this up in order to be one of two, or even worse, one of four?

Not to be minimised too is the fact that without adequate safety measures, one is asking contending leaders between whom little love is lost to reside together within Cambodia, the sheep to lie down with the wolves. There is the small matter of ensuring sheer physical survival. (This is why there is so much revolving around the desire to see a lot of [international or national] shepherds, with sticks of some size, shepherds furthermore who can and will use their sticks).

Fourth, and by far the greatest obstacle to national reconciliation at this stage, is the fact that whilst all share some common nationalist aspirations, each remains intent on pursuing personal and factional interests. Each of the four factions have their own vital interests. None are prepared to sacrifice them to the vital interests of the fifth faction — the Cambodian people.

And because there is suspicion about whether the universally touted process of national self determination can be fair or will even be implemented in the end, it is around the issue of power-sharing that three-quarters of the problems of reaching a negotiated agreement between the internal players will revolve at this stage. The major outstanding issues — the structure and functioning of the 'interim' administering authority, the international control mechanism, disarmament of the fighting forces, the forms and processes of self determination, and all the questions of sequencing — can all be expected to be connected with the fundamental question of power-sharing.

The Hun Sen regime's priority at this stage is patently clear: divide and rule. Its maximalist and present intent is to construct what in alliance theory is called 'the minimum winning coalition', co-opting *just enough* allies to allow it to 'win', thus ensuring that it shares as little power as possible. The top priority option is to co-opt Prince Sihanouk as mostly a figurehead and to absorb FUNCINCPEC (National United Front for an Independent, Neutral, Peaceful and Cooperative

Cambodia) if the costs are minimal. With a generally powerless prince at the head of a problematical Supreme Council and an act of self determination to be carried out under the auspices of the council but by the Hun Sen adminstrative apparatus ('who else is there to do the job?') it is gambling on a full and legitimised election to power. Under this arrangement, and without the political albatross of the Vietnamese troops around its neck, the Hun Sen regime is supremely confident that in a relatively peaceful and 'fair' election to be conducted within months of Vietnamese withdrawal, they will triumph.

The KPNLF strategy is also clear. Since it is by far the weakest faction, it is naturally intent on ensuring the establishment of a quadripartite government. Full stop.

Prince Sihanouk's present preferences are also quite plain. First, he would like to stand above the fray and above the four parties, thus becoming in effect the fifth party. He would be the fifth force, able to hold sway and be the final arbiter. Thus the preference (if possible) for four of everything: four ministers for every ministry, four armies, a system of government that would ensure perpetual deadlock — and thus a constant reference to the prince.

The Khmer Rouge's strategies are harder to discern and prove. But it would not be surprising if it feels constrained to go along with the political game whilst maintaining all its military options. The amount of popular electoral support it can secure in reasonably free and fair elections will surprise most analysts. But it cannot hope to secure power through the ballot box and must continue to hold on to the bayonet. Should a political process of national reconciliation be secured or knocked together, with a lot of external actors doing the knocking, the Khmer Rouge is by no means the only faction capable of adopting a dual track strategy.

III. Six endgame scenarios on Cambodia

Given this pattern of positive and negative fundamentals, it is not surprising that movement has been greatest at the level of the external conflict. But given all the factors, and events yet to come, what are some (of the very many possible) endgame scenarios for the Cambodia conflict?

There is need for intellectual humility. Strange things have happened of late and even stranger things may be in train. But one clear possibility is what might be called the 'Sideshow Scenario'.

The Sideshow Scenario

According to this scenario, the external actors proceed to a resolution of the international dimension of the conflict and more or less wash their hands of the whole matter, leaving the internal actors to sort things out. In terms of international relations, Cambodia becomes a sideshow, out of mind, and with the assistance of the international media, out of sight.

Vietnamese troops will leave by September 30 — or for dramatic effect even before then — leaving behind perhaps a few hundred advisors. All four internal players can be left to fend for themselves. The Khmer Rouge can start the fighting again. (Everyone seems to be puzzlingly agreed that they have enough supplies for 'two' years. The fighting could go on for substantially longer in fact). China need do nothing (although many doubt that this is what China will do). The Soviet Union and Vietnam can cut the war-related assistance to the Hun Sen regime.

This could be a partial solution in itself. Threatening it or implementing it could also be a means for forcing an internal resolution of the conflict. The most likely shorter term outcome would be continued fighting (which cannot be referred to as a 'civil war' since a civil war is one where large populations are militarily invaded). Or there could be a tripartite coalition, with Prince Sihanouk and Son Sann and their factions playing various types of roles within a Hun Sen-dominated administration.

Without having to necessarily agree, it might be useful here to quote what Vietnamese Foreign Minister Nguyen Co Thach said on August 30, 1988 in an interview with the Vietnam News Agency:

> There are many complicated problems which could not be solved promptly. Therefore, the settlement of the international aspect first, then the internal aspect later, becomes *the most possible reality*. There are many precedents for resolving the international aspects first in the Laos settlement in 1961-62 and the Afghanistan issue in 1988. Though there are similarities and differences as well in the Lao, Afghan and Kampuchean issues, we hold that if the international aspect is settled first, the Kampuchean issue will no longer be the difference between countries in the region but only the difference of Kampuchea. If so this will benefit the safeguarding of peace and the development of friendship and cooperation in Southeast Asia thus conforming to the long-term interests of all nations in the region.

The Informal Disengagement Scenario

It might however be argued that at this stage there would remain problems that may not be explicitly and formally resolvable, even at the international level. This being so, it is possible to conceptualise a second scenario which might be called the 'Informal (Gradualist) External Disengagement Scenario' whereby the external players gradually reduce their participation, in keeping with what is likely to be increasing disinterest in full engagement. This does not require the external actors even to meet to reach a formal agreement between themselves. It could be conducted on the basis of a process of unilateral reciprocative disengagement.

The No Political Reconciliation Scenario

A third 'No Political Reconciliation Scenario' could arise if there is no internal reconciliation and no international settlement. This would be a perpetuation of the present status quo. Some factors such as the diversion of Chinese foreign policy might suggest the likelihood of this scenario, which is not without its virtues. (It is to be noted that it would be a perpetuation of the present status quo without Vietnamese troops and without de-escalated Khmer Rouge military activities should the Khmer Rouge decide to resume the military offensive after Vietnamese troop withdrawal).[1]

The Hun Sen-Plus Scenario

A fourth scenario could come from resolution of the international 'aspects' and 'partial' resolution of the internal 'aspects', if, for example, the Hun Sen regime and the Sihanoukists (and possibly the KPNLF) succeed in coming to an agreement among themselves. This might be called the 'Hun Sen-Plus Scenario'.[2]

The Comprehensive Solution Scenario

A fifth scenario is the 'Comprehensive Solution Scenario', the successful conclusion of what is now being tried.

---

1.   At a recent discussion with an ISIS delegation, Hun Sen said: 'The fourth possibility, there will be no political solution. It is not good at all. But if the situation forces us to accept this situation, we have no way but to accept it. If there is no political solution, it will be very bad but also it will be worse for Prince Sihanouk. I would like to tell you that with or without a political solution, after September 30, there will be no Vietnamese troops in Cambodia. So far, you have allied yourself to fight against us under the pretext of fighting the Vietnamese. Now, after September what will be your pretext? After September, if there is a civil war, there is support from outside countries, then it will be the responsibility of these countries and not ours anymore. I can tell you that the Khmer Rouge, Pol Potists have no chance of grabbing power from us because they enjoy no support from the population. And Prince Sihanouk cannot benefit from the situation like it was from 1970-75. So the weak point of Prince Sihanouk is his alliance with the Khmer Rouge. He has not developed his political and military forces inside the country in this regard. On the contrary, we started from scratch, now we have built up our own forces, we fought against the Khmer Rouge and for this reason the people supported us. But without a political solution, it is bad for us because that means the war will continue. But we cannot prolong the presence of the Vietnamese troops beyond September of this year, therefore we will withdraw the Vietnamese troops without any political solution'. *An Informal Exchange of Views on Cambodia*, Monday, May 15, 1989, Phnom Penh, Cambodia, pp26-27.

2.   Hun Sen calls this the 'four-wheel cart formula': 'The two front wheels will represent the alliance between Prince Sihanouk and myself and the two rear wheels will represent Mr Son Sann and the Khmer Rouge. Prince Sihanouk has already recognised our constitution and he only asked us to amend a few more articles of the constitution. The two front wheels will act as a motor dragging the other two stubborn ones to come along. We should not allow the Khmer Rouge to veto everything. I told Prince Sihanouk that he should not allow the Khmer Rouge to veto Prince Sihanouk's policy or veto the other factions' policy. We do not drop them out completely but we cannot receive them altogether in a whole and we cannot allow them to play the vital role when the lives and the deaths of the people are at stake. Right now the alliance between us and Prince Sihanouk is very important in a political settlement as well as in the event of preventing the regime of Pol Pot. In the event of a political solution, the alliance will act as the dragnet to drag the other parties into the election. If the Khmer Rouge would like to continue to work, I believe this alliance of ours could prevent them from doing so.' *An Informal Exchange of Views on Cambodia, op cit*, p24-25.

The Back to the Beginning Scenario

A sixth scenario is a return to the middle game of the early to mid-1980s, stalemate at a relatively high level of external engagement and internal conflict.

All six scenarios are possible, significantly, with the last perhaps least likely.

IV. Necessary or extremely useful components of the process of (maximalist) comprehensive political settlement

At this stage, it is premature to abandon the struggle for a comprehensive political settlement. It might be argued that the following are necessary or extremely useful elements of such a maximalist solution.

First and foremost, the total withdrawal of all Vietnamese military troops.

Second, a military ceasefire or a less formal 'standstill' on all sides; and the establishment of internal law and order and security.

Third, the gradual reduction of all military assistance to all present Cambodian parties and, with the total withdrawal of Vietnamese armed forces, the complete termination of all military assistance to all present and future Cambodian parties.

Fourth, the establishment of a provisional coalition authority which is subordinate to no other authority (headed by Prince Sihanouk) and with quadripartite representation.

Fifth, the establishment of a standing international conference.

Sixth, the introduction of an effective international control mechanism. (The December 1988 Chinese-Soviet statement states that: 'The Chinese and Soviet sides consider it necessary and important for an effective international control mechanism to be established and [to] exercise strict international supervision over Vietnamese troop withdrawal, cessation of foreign military aid, maintenance of peace in Kampuchea and conduct of free elections').

Seventh, the exercise of self determination of the Cambodian people through reasonably free, fair and legitimate elections.

Eighth, the establishment of an international guarantee for the status of Cambodia as a sovereign, independent, non-aligned, neutral, peaceful, stable, unthreatening and unpartitioned state.

Ninth, the achievement of a minimum level of national reconciliation.

Tenth, the establishment of safeguards against the return of the Khmer Rouge to dominant power and against the return of genocidal policies.

Eleventh, the repatriation of Cambodian refugees.

Twelfth, the establishment of an association of all Southeast Asian states.

V. Areas of disagreement or unclear answers

There are still areas of disagreement and many questions with regard to many of these elements of a comprehensive settlement of the Cambodian conflict.

With regard to *Vietnamese withdrawal,* there was some confusion after JIM II. However, the April 5 reiteration by Vietnam that all its remaining troops will withdraw 'with or without a political settlement' has cleared the air, at least in declaratory terms. A June 4 statement in Bangkok stated that Vietnam planned to complete troop withdrawal by September 15. The withdrawal is to be carried out in two phases: the initial phase involving heavy arms, engineering and construction units, started in May, will be completed in July; phase two involves the main combat units.[3]

Nevertheless, there are still questions as to whether Vietnamese advisors will still be present. And there have been allegations that many troops will simply be changing uniforms.

With regard to the question of a ceasefire and the *establishment of law, order and security* in Cambodia, how is this to be done? Specifically, what will be the position with regard to the armed forces of the four factions?

In a July 7, 1988 statement on 'National Reconciliation Policy' made public by Hun Sen at a press conference in Fere-en-Tarendois, it was stated: 'From now until the general election is held it is imperative that...The political and military status quo in Cambodia be maintained; the armed forces of all sides should stay where they are stationed, refrain from moving to other places and cease all hostile military activities. The founding of the Cambodian state's armed forces in the future shall be considered and decided upon by the government appointed following the general election.' This position has remained firm.

According to the Text of Address of Prince Sihanouk to Representatives of the Four Cambodian Factions attending the Bogor Talks (July 27, 1988), Prince Sihanouk proposed that: 'We keep intact our four armies but they fraternally form the national army of Cambodia (quadripartite national army) with a quadripartite general staff (collegial).'

Over a Voice of the Khmer broadcast on October 18, 1988, Son Soubert of the

---

3.   However, many observers still believe that the withdrawal is still linked to the cessation of external military aid to the three Khmer resistance parties as well as an end to foreign interference in Cambodia (*Far Eastern Economic Review,* April 20, 1989, P10; *The Nation,* April 19, 1989). The People's Republic of China is not fully convinced of Vietnam's intention. The PRC's position on this issue is that if all Vietnamese troops are actually withdrawn from Cambodia, China will end all military aid. For this to materialise, there must be reliable verification (*The Nation,* May 15 & 17, 1989). And in the absence of such verification, China will continue to insist on its three principles, namely: there must be a political solution with, as a precondition, a genuine and complete withdrawal of Vietnamese troops from Cambodia; authority in Cambodia should be a quadripartite coalition government headed by Prince Sihanouk, which should be internationally guaranteed; and a political settlement must be accompanied by elimination of elements which may lead to civil war (*Far Eastern Economic Review,* March 30, 1989, p 27).

KPNLF argued: 'First, ... we must disarm all parties and create an equally represented police and security force, and second, that this Cambodian police and security force must assist the international peace-keeping force.'

China's position was clearly stated in a Foreign Ministry statement issued on July 1, 1988: 'Upon the establishment of the provisional quadripartite government of Kampuchea, a freeze should be imposed on Kampuchean forces of all factions and those forces should refrain from getting involved in politics and interfering in the general election so that the Kampuchean people may conduct a free election without outside interference and threat of force.'

In October 1988, China's Foreign Minister, Qian Qichen stated in point three of a five-point statement in the UN General Assembly: 'As soon as the provisional coalition government is established, a freeze should be imposed on the armed forces of all factions and they should not be involved in politics or free elections. To prevent civil war, the armed forces of all factions may be disbanded to facilitate creation of a unified national defence force. It would be composed of an equal number of officers and men of all four factions under a unified command.'

The proposals made by the Khmer Rouge seem to be also most interesting. In Democratic Kampuchea's Proposal for a Comprehensive Political Solution to the Cambodian Problem, dated August 15, 1988, the Khmer Rouge proposed that: 'In the last phase of the withdrawal of the SRV forces from Cambodia... put the armed forces of each Cambodian party in garrisons under the control and supervision of a four-party Cambodian committee and under international control and supervision.'

In an August 15, 1988 broadcast over the Voice of the National Army of Democratic Kampuchea, the Khmer Rouge stated: 'Democratic Kampuchea believes that the size of each party's army should be fixed at only 10,000 men. The reasons are as follows:

(1) This number is appropriate to the post-war situation;
(2) There would be an international guarantee;
(3) There would be a treaty of friendship and non-aggression between Cambodia and the SRV and Southeast Asian countries;
(4) Fixing the size of each party's army at this number would reduce any eventual clashes between the armed forces of the four parties.'

(One question of course is what happens to the 'surplus' troops).

In the same broadcast, the Khmer Rouge made known its national defence policy dated March 8, 1987, which had called for the following arrangements: 'All national forces must consult on the organisation of a single national army which is under the control of the defence ministry, under the command of a single national supreme command, under the management of a single general staff, and which obeys and performs its duties according to a single code and command.'

With regard to the third element, it is to be noted that everyone is agreed that the external assistance that should be terminated is 'military assistance', which means that money can easily move in to each of the factions. Quite clearly, financial assistance for arms purchases, etc, would be a violation of the spirit but not of the letter of the agreement on the *cessation of external military assistance* to all the factions.

With regard to the fourth element, the *establishment of a provisional coalition authority*, it is important to quote the December 1988 PRC-Soviet statement: 'The Chinese side stands for the establishment of a provisional coalition government in Kampuchea headed by Prince Sihanouk and with quadripartite representation'.

The joint statement also stated that 'the Soviet side will support an agreement among the four parties in Kampuchea on the establishment of a provisional organ under the charge of Sihanouk and with quadripartite representation. This organ should not be subordinate to any party in Kampuchea and its task is to implement agreements reached by the parties in Kampuchea and to conduct free elections'.

It is quite clear that the Chinese and the CGDK want a quadripartite interim government, which would mean the double dissolution of the CGDK and the PRK at the same time and their replacement by a provisional quadripartite government.

The Hun Sen position is as follows: 'We have proposed to maintain the political and military status quo until the result of the election. In order to organise the election, we propose to set up the *Supreme Council* of leaders. This body will be independent from all the parties. And we can propose Prince Sihanouk as Chairman of this Council and a number of deputy chairmen from the other parties. It can have its seat in Phnom Penh here and also the assistance and protection from the International Control Commission (ICC). This Council will be given the duty to conduct and to implement all the agreements that have been reached between the Cambodian parties. And it also will have the duty to draft the electoral rules and to oversee the other process of the elections. It will conduct and organise elections. It will also draft the new constitution to be submitted to the new national assembly. Then we can proceed to elections under effective international control. So once the new government has been elected, my government here and the CGDK will automatically dissolve. The same thing will apply to military matters. We maintain the military status quo until the election and before that we will have a ceasefire until the outcome of the election. After the election, the new government will have the duty to reorganise the national army — whether to dissolve or to merge all of them, it is up to the new government to undertake.'[4]

This entire question might be reduced in importance somewhat if there is a very short gap between the establishment of an interim authority and the holding of general elections, which will elect the new government. But there are too many unbelievers as to whether this can or will happen. And this question would appear to be very hard to dissolve as the Hun Sen regime will not be prepared to be dismantled, lock, stock and barrel.

How is this serious problem to be resolved? Theoretically, it might be possible to dismiss all present employees of the Hun Sen regime for, say, 24 hours, to establish a new supra body and then to legally re-employ all former employees.

---

4.   *An Informal Exchange of Views on Cambodia, op cit*, p19-20.

But some have argued that the only practical compromise is the establishment of a four party collegial entity at the ministerial and deputy-ministerial level, which would be superimposed over what is already there: policemen, postmen, firemen, teachers, clerks etc.

The fifth question — *the international conference* — appears one of the easiest to resolve. According to Hun Sen: 'We agreed with Prince Sihanouk on the venue of the conference, that Jakarta and Paris should be the alternate venues. During my courtesy call on President Suharto, he also accepted this proposal. We have proposed the participants to the conference as follows: the six Asean countries, Laos and Vietnam, the five permanent members of the United Nations Security Council (the United States, China, France, Britain and the USSR), the chairmen of the sixth, seventh and eighth Non-aligned Summits, the United Nations Secretary-General and also a number of other countries which contribute to the settlement of the problem of Cambodia. Prince Sihanouk proposed to add Australia, New Zealand and Japan — I believe this is not a problem, we can include them. We have a few worries with regard to Japan but we do not want to exclude them, because in the international conference or in any meeting, we should not create a confrontational atmosphere. Japan has been on one side, it is difficult if one country is [on] one side. So even in a football match, you must get a neutral referee. Then the question was asked, why [do] we allow the Asean countries to take part? Well, the Asean countries are in the region. The Asean countries recognised the CGDK but we admit that the Asean countries are in the region and can take part in the solution. China has been opposing us but China is acceptable because China is a member of the United Nations Security Council. Japan is not a country in our region and is not a member of the United Nations Security Council. But I think Japan could take part.'[5]

Among the remaining questions is whether Canada should be invited and also the other countries which have and can contribute to the settlement of the problem of Cambodia. Is it also clear that what everyone envisages is an international conference that would meet even after 'the settlement', useful perhaps to discuss post-settlement developments and in the context of international guarantees?

The sixth question is the issue of an *effective international mechanism*. The CGDK have proposed an International Control Commission (to which all are agreed) *and* an International Peace Keeping Force (to which the Hun Sen regime and the Vietnamese are not). It would appear possible to resolve this disagreement by not referring to any International Peace Keeping Force, but to give the International Control Commission to which all are agreed, a helmeted arm. The CGDK has asked for such a force to be 2,000 strong.

The view of Hun Sen is as follows: 'In 1954, the International Control Commission was made up of 60 persons when they came to control Cambodia. I think we must have an appropriate number. If we think of now, we must have 10 times the number. That means it could increase to 600 persons. Of course, if all the

---

5.   *An Informal Exchange of Views on Cambodia, op cit*, p32-33.

600 wanted to they could have small arms. At the same time we propose to set up a Cambodian Quadripartite Control Commission to work together with the International Control Commission. Therefore the numbers will be sufficient to have effective control.'[6]

All are agreed on the functions of the ICC. As to the membership of the ICC, which participants at this Asia-Pacific Roundtable might discuss to good effect, it is the view of the Hun Sen regime that: 'With regard to the International Control Commission, we agreed with Prince Sihanouk to let the international conference decide. And we seem to agree on the earlier formula of six countries — two socialist countries, two non-aligned countries and two western countries, so we should let the international conference determine the International Control Commission. I like also to inform Your Excellency that Prince Sihanouk has dropped this demand to send into Cambodia the United Nations peace-keeping force. We also have dropped our proposal to send in the 1954 International Control Commission. So we should come to a middle formula and let the international conference decide. Although the International Control Commission team is without any army, we have given thought to providing them with means to defend themselves. So we proposed that they could be armed with small, light weapons for self-defence and for the performance of their mission.'[7]

With regard to the *exercise of self determination,* all are agreed that the ICC should adopt an observation and reporting role and the modalities and the conduct be done by an authority under Prince Sihanouk. The difference is that the Hun Sen regime, Vietnam and the USSR want the authority to be under a Supreme Council. The CGDK and China want it to be under a provisional quadripartite government.

There are a great many nuts and bolts issues related to the conduct of elections. But quite obviously, on practical grounds, elections will have to be

---

6.   According to Hun Sen: 'With regard to the Cambodian Quadripartite Control Commission, it will be decided by the Cambodian parties themselves and if the Supreme Council could be set up, of course that Quadripartite Supreme Council would decide. With regard to the size of the Cambodian Commission, it could be negotiable and it will have to perform its mission alongside the International Control Commission. With regard to the pros and cons of the size of the International Control Commission, I believe that if it is too small, it is not good either and if it is too big, it is not good either. I would like to tell Your Excellencies that during our talks at JIM II, there were discusssions on this matter. At one of our discussions with the Asean Foreign Ministers and especially with the Singapore Minister of Foreign Affairs, he insisted on the sending of the United Nations Peace-Keeping Force to Cambodia. So, I asked him "whether you send this team to Cambodia to fight the war or to control the situation?" I remember very well that day. The Minister of Foreign Affairs of Singapore as well as His Excellency Foreign Minister Omar said unanimously: "No, we are not going to fight the war". I said that in that case, if we go and make the control therefore we must be prepared for the mission of the control. We have 300,000 militiamen already, therefore I think the size that we proposed for the International Control Commission together with the Cambodian Control Commission would be adequate enough to control the situation, because our country is very small. In 1954 we had only 60 persons [in the International Control Commission], so now we multiply [that number by] 10 to 600.' *An Informal Exchange of Views on Cambodia, op cit,* p35-36.

7.   *An Informal Exchange of Views on Cambodia, op cit,* p33-34.

administered by the administrative infrastructure now in place. (This Hun Sen administrative structure is not as committed to Hun Sen as many may presume). And there is agreement at this stage that elections will choose a Constituent Assembly, which shall draft a constitution and choose a government. There is also agreement that all 'parties' should be allowed to run in the elections, although it is the view of the Hun Sen regime that 'war criminals' should not be allowed to stand for election.

It is Hun Sen's suggestion that elections be held three months after the complete withdrawal of the Vietnamese. There is the view that if a substantial time were to elapse, Prince Sihanouk and the Sihanoukists will be able to perform better at the polls. It has also been pointed out that Cambodia has little experience with free and fair elections.

With regard to *international guarantees,* there could be several issues including whether they shall be individually undertaken but with no provision with regard to action by any member of the international conference or the conference as a whole; or with provisions for individual and/or collective action in the event of a violation.

As to content, the state of Cambodia could:

- Undertake not to introduce foreign troops, military advisors or personnel, armaments, ammunition and other war materials into Cambodia under any form whatsoever, and not to tolerate the introduction of troops, military advisors and personnel, armaments, ammunition and other war materials into Cambodia by any foreign country;
- Undertake not to establish military bases in Cambodia and not to tolerate the establishment of foreign military bases in Cambodia in any form whatsoever;
- Undertake not to bring Cambodia into any military or political alliance for whatever reason;
- Undertake not to use the territory of Cambodia to conduct activities directly or indirectly aimed at another state; and
- Generally undertake to guarantee Cambodia's position as a sovereign, independent, nonaligned, neutral, peaceful and stable country.

The external guarantors could:

- Undertake not to introduce troops, military advisors or personnel, armaments, ammunition and other war materials into Cambodia under any form whatsoever;
- Undertake not to establish military bases in Cambodia;
- Undertake not to enter into any military or political alliance with Cambodia;
- Undertake not to use the territory of Cambodia to conduct activities directly or indirectly aimed at another country; and
- Generally undertake to respect the sovereignty, independence, non-aligned status, neutrality and territorial integrity of Cambodia.

With regard to achieving a minimum level of necessary *national reconcili-*

ation, all are in declaratory terms agreed on its need. But enormous problems remain in the way.

With regard to the *establishment of safeguards* against the return of the Khmer Rouge to dominant power and against the possible return of genocidal policies, on both of which the PRC and everyone else (including the Khmer Rouge) are agreed *in their public statements*, what can be done? Is it sufficient to ensure that a list of say, 20 persons (or more), five from each of the four factions, be excluded from any governmental post? Can this be negotiated? Would China and Vietnam and the four factions be able to agree?

With regard to the repatriation of *Cambodian refugees*, the problem is not as simple as it may look. It is agreed that the power bases of the three CGDK factions are deeply connected with how the refugees are repatriated and where they are repatriated. Can we agree with the Hun Sen formulation of November 8, 1988: 'All refugees temporarily living in neighbouring countries may be repatriated on their own free will. The repatriates shall enjoy the full rights of other Kampuchean citizens, and participate in national reconciliation and national construction. The repatriation will be arranged through consultations with the countries concerned and with assistance from international organisations'. Is this one area where the UN can play a dominant role?

It is the argument of many that in order to ensure a solution that is viable in the longer term, it is important that Cambodia and the other states of Southeast Asia be part of either Asean or preferably, of a *new association of Southeast Asian states.*

This paper started with a rather bold statement: that the game of conflict in and over Cambodia which started at the end of 1978 will in all likelihood end before the end of 1989. The bold assertion might be justified because after Vietnamese withdrawal and the events that will come over the next few months, it indeed is most likely that the game of conflict in Cambodia and over Cambodia will not be *quite* the same.

There can be little doubt that the Cambodian endgame will be a very protracted one. It is important that in this protracted endgame the greatest attention should be devoted — for the first time — to the fifth faction, the long-suffering Cambodian people who must be given hope and peace.

Beyond Cambodia: Some thoughts on Southeast Asia in the 1990s

SUKHUMBHAND PARIBATRA
Director, Institute of Security and International Studies, Chulalongkorn University, Thailand

Introduction

THE assigned brief for this paper is to explore 'specific proposals to create a framework for peace and security in Southeast Asia' in what has been termed, perhaps rather optimistically at this juncture, the 'post-Cambodia era'. The task is by no means an easy one. Firstly, all proposals are normative and hence ultimately subjective, being inseparable from the proposers' own beliefs and values, norms and prejudices, which may not be shared by others. Secondly, the relevance and the credibility of a given proposal pertaining to the future are ultimately dependent, not upon the intrinsic merits of that proposal, but upon the future itself, the unfolding of which is uncertain and unpredictable.

Given these constraints, the task to be attempted here is necessarily a modest one, that is, to put forward some ideas concerning the possible ways and means of enhancing Southeast Asia's peace and security as the end of the 20th century approaches, so that these ideas can serve to provoke further thoughts and discussions on the matter. As stated above, proposals are formulated ultimately upon the basis of the proposers' own beliefs and values, norms and prejudices. Therefore, at this juncture before one engages in discussing the matter at hand, it may be pertinent to spell out the author's own assumptions and prejudices.

Firstly, it is believed that in the long term Southeast Asia's peace and security are indivisible, that one cannot render the whole peaceful and secure by striving to make only parts thereof peaceful and secure.

Secondly, it is believed that in order to make Southeast Asia peaceful and secure, the region must be transformed into one where all the states within it are willing and are given opportunities to live, deal and interact with one another in mutually beneficial ways, free from great power military interventions in any form. Furthermore, it is also believed that to be peaceful and secure, all of Southeast Asia must be prosperous or given a chance of becoming prosperous, which in turn requires that all regional states be provided access to global markets and global sources of capital, technology and services.

Thirdly, it is believed that long-term peace and security in Southeast Asia can be attained, not through rash, indiscriminate or premature surrender to idealism and idealistic notions (for example, unilateral disarmament), but through admixtures of idealism, pragmatism and realistic appraisals of what is and will be. In this connection, it is believed that a region-wide order is a *sine qua non* of Southeast Asia's long-term peace and security and that this region-wide order could and should be constructed along the lines successfully pioneered by the Association of Southeast Asian Nations (Asean) — that is, an order built partly on commonsense and partly on consensus upon, and strict adherence to, principles, norms and rules of the game concerning independence, sovereignty, non-intervention, non-aggression, and pacific settlement of disputes. It is also believed that Asean's ideas of transforming Southeast Asia into a Zone of Peace, Freedom and Neutrality (or ZOPFAN) and a nuclear-weapons-free zone are valuable, not as ideals to be strictly adhered to or rigid concepts to be put into operation within a short or specific period of time, but as general aspirations to guide one's efforts to enhance regional peace and security over time.

As also stated above, proposals cannot be formulated in a vacuum. Therefore, before attempting the task, one should first try to assess and predict as best as one can the major trends likely to take place over the next several years, both at the global and at the regional levels, which have a bearing upon Southeast Asia's peace and security.

Trends

There seems to be three major trends taking place at the global level which have and will continue to have a bearing on the future of Southeast Asia.

The first trend is the continued growth of interdependence in the international system.

With the rapid development and proliferation of the technologies of peace and war as well as the rapid expansion of social, economic and technological linkages across political boundaries, all nations of this world have become and will continue to be increasingly interdependent in their fates — in both their security and their well-being. This growth of interdependence will certainly remain a highly uneven process involving some nations more than others. But by the end of this century the international system in many ways will more and more be, and will be recognised to be, a community of shared vulnerabilities and shared interests.

Partly as a consequence of this process of growing interdependence, the state's capacity to be master and lord of its own future and its own destiny will continue to diminish. Willy-nilly, the state has to deal with external developments and to respond to external stimuli. Socialist countries are by no means immune to this 'opening-up' process, and social and economic autarchies increasingly have to adjust themselves to the new realities of having to cope with the outside world, to recognise that there is life beyond their national boundaries which they have to live with and attach importance to.

The second global trend is the increased priority being attached to economics and economic matters in relations amongst states and in the governance of nations.

There is little doubt that politics is and will be of paramount importance in many issue areas, especially national security. But there seems to be an increasingly strong consensus, cutting across all lines of political, ideological and socio-economic divide, that economic well-being is a *sine qua non* of a nation's security. Accordingly, throughout the international system the task of promoting or protecting economic prosperity is likely to become more and more the focus of national policy.

In this context the major industrialised countries will increasingly expend their energies on seeking ways and means of maintaining their economic predominance and also of managing the stresses and strains caused by the process of transformation into post-industrial societies. Some will rely upon unilateral measures, as in the case of the United States, and others will focus upon multilateral approaches, especially economic bloc-building. Non-communist developing nations will increasingly attempt to enhance their economic performance and accelerate their economic development, both in conflict and in cooperation with industrialised countries. Socialist countries will more and more likely see ideological steadfastness as the main obstacle and economic pragmatism as the main key to progress.

While the growing importance of economics has proved to be beneficial in that it has led to a decrease of geostrategic and ideological rivalry among states, as will be elaborated below, it has also helped to make economic competition once more a crucial dimension of international politics. Trade wars have so far been avoided but the continued rise of protectionist sentiments, especially in industrialised countries, means that more, rather than less, global tension is likely to be generated by trade and trade-related concerns in the near future.

The third global trend is continued diminution of conflict and tension in the politics among nations.

Growing interdependence, together with increasing concern with economics, has helped to bring about rapprochement and detente in almost all adversary relationships. In this context the most dramatic developments have taken place in great power relations. The United States and the Soviet Union have once more reverted to the path of dialogues, arms control and management of differences on the question of regional conflicts. The Soviet Union and China have removed most of the obstacles in the path towards full normalisation of their bilateral relations.

The process of great power rapprochement may prove to be an uneven one. It may be hampered by a number of factors, for example domestic problems in China, the Soviet Union or an Eastern European country, and deterioration of the situations in Southern Africa or the Middle East. But on the whole it may be reasonable to predict that the domestic priorities of the great powers, especially the enormity of their economic problems, will lead to a continuation of this process — the 1990s will witness more arms control agreements and significant reductions of the global military presence of the great powers, thus further helping to make the politics among nations at the regional level much more free of tension and conflict than in the mid-1970s and the early 1980s.

More specifically where Southeast Asia is concerned, a number of inter-related trends are emerging or are about to emerge which may bring about significant changes in the relations among major powers in the region, in the relations between major powers and regional states, and also in the relations among regional states themselves.

One trend which may be about to emerge clearly is the propensity on the part of the United States, the Soviet Union and China to reduce their respective strategic commitments related to Southeast Asia.

In a context where there is a low level of global tension, preoccupation with domestic economic priorities is likely to exert constant pressure on the American and Soviet superpowers to streamline their armed forces and to limit their military presence in the region. In the case of the United States, this propensity will in all probability be accentuated by the Philippines' continued reluctance to allow the Americans to use its bases for too lengthy a period of time after 1991. In the case of the Soviet Union, the propensity to reduce its military burdens is likely to be strengthened by the termination of Vietnam's military intervention in Cambodia and Hanoi's desire to reach out to the non-communist world, concerning which there will be further discussion below. Where China is concerned, preoccupation with domestic economic priorities, successful rapprochement with the Soviet Union and continuing uncertainty that is bound to emanate from the recent political turmoil are likely to induce a low military profile in Southeast Asia on the part of Beijing, except where the South China Sea is concerned, as will also be discussed below.

Another trend is the growing recognition of the importance of economics on the part of regional states.

Recognition of the importance of economics is not a new phenomenon in Southeast Asia. Indeed the non-communist states of the region belonging to Asean have identified economic development as being an integral part of the process of promoting what they term 'national' and 'regional' resilience. But what seems to be unprecedented is the extent of this recognition.

In the first place, Southeast Asian states which had generally shunned or been equivocal about their full participation in the global economic development process have more readily accepted the importance of such participation. Burma is in the process of opening up and by the early 1990s it may be much more involved in the world economic system. But it is in Indochina that dramatic changes have taken place.

Vietnam had for a long time been prepared to undergo economic deprivation for the sake of its national security and had defied sanctions imposed by most of its neighbours and most of the industrialised nations against its military occupation of Cambodia. Even when economic reforms were attempted in the early 1980s, Hanoi had refused to accept that the logic of these reforms should lead to a reappraisal of its Cambodia policy which had brought about Vietnam's economic isolation. But from the mid-1980s, a combination of pressure from its Soviet ally and recognition of the dire straits its economy was in prompted Vietnam to be much more yielding where Cambodia was concerned. It is no coincidence that successive announcements of unilateral withdrawal from Cambodia have been accompanied by renewed efforts to attract foreign trade and investment. Both Laos and the People's Republic of Kampuchea (PRK) regime in Phnom Penh have also attempted to reach out to the outside world in a similar manner. Indeed when PRK Prime Minister Hun Sen visited Bangkok in January and May 1989, exchanges with the Thai private sector were specifically requested by him and his party.

Secondly, recognition of the importance of economics has also brought about dramatic changes in Thailand's Indochina policy.

When Chatichai Choonhavan became prime minister in August 1989, he announced his intention to transform Indochina 'from a battlefield into a trading market'. In subsequent months he had not only made many conciliatory moves towards the three Indochinese countries but also encouraged the Thai private sector to trade with and invest in Vietnam and Laos, and given the 'green light' for informal trade ties with the PRK. A large infrastructural and industrial development programme has been formulated for the northeastern region of Thailand, in part to serve as a base for increasing and conducting economic ties with Indochina.

The manner that this so-called 'New Diplomacy' has been brought about might have been somewhat abrupt, thus taking many of Thailand's friends and allies by surprise. But the 'New Diplomacy' is based upon firmly-rooted beliefs on the part of Chatichai and upon long-term trends taking place in Thailand.

Where the prime minister is concerned, extensive experience as a diplomat and industrialist-financier has taught Chatichai that economics is a great healer of wounds: Increased economic ties help to draw adversaries together, assist in the task of managing conflict between them in the short term, and strengthen the fabric of peace in the longer term. As he said in a Keynote Address to the Conference on 'Indochina: From War Zone to Trade Zone', organised by *The Nation* and *The Asian Wall Street Journal* in Bangkok on April 28, 1989:

Let me put it very simply and tell this distinguished audience one thing: that I am a simple man and I like simple home truths.

The first home truth is that in wars there are no winners.

The second home truth is that common prosperity is the best guarantee of peace.

In the world we live in, wars cannot be ruled out and there can be no simple preventive cure for armed conflicts among states. But when nations and people trade with one another, when nations and peoples invest in one another's land, when nations and peoples interact with one another across a broad spectrum of economic endeavours, and when nations and peoples enjoy mutual benefits from these endeavours, they have little incentive to bear arms against one another....

I believe that all regional states must participate fully in the process of economic development, that they must engage in mutually beneficial exchanges so that the fruits of economic development are shared. For in the last resort common prosperity is the best guarantee against armed hostilities.

Moreover, Prime Minister Chatichai also believes that, given the present world economic trends, Thailand's best interests lie in diversification of economic ties. Although the Indochinese markets can never substitute for markets elsewhere, Thailand must gain access to them as a necessary part of this diversification process.

Chatichai's overtures towards Indochina have been well supported by most of the political parties and the business community in Thailand. For one thing the growth of the Thai parliamentary system has allowed the business community to have greater participation, through the political parties, parliament, and ministerial portfolios, in making decisions — mostly on foreign policy — which had until now been the exclusive preserve of the bureaucrats. Thus it is probably inevitable that economic considerations have become more important in foreign policy. With the rapid pace of Thailand's economic growth, both accomplished and projected, most of the private sector has been prompted to see in Indochina an opportunity to maintain this economic performance, especially since Indochina is thought to be a potential supplier of many raw materials needed by Thailand, including timber, precious stones, iron and coal.

In Southeast Asia politics and personalities are not easily separable. Changes of leadership in Indochina and Thailand may conceivably reverse the present policy directions. On the other hand these policies seem to be rooted in longer-term factors and indeed are paralleled by trends elsewhere in the international system. Thus it may be reasonable to expect that they will persist even if leadership changes take place, as they must over time.

The third major trend is the continued emergence of what may be termed 'non-traditional' security issues. With the rapid rate of utilisation, and depletion, of natural resources in Southeast Asia, it is perhaps inevitable that resource-related issues will increasingly become important security concerns.

The question of the South China Sea with its hydrocarbon resources is perhaps the most crucial. There are many overlapping claims in the area and one of the claimants is a great power, the People's Republic of China, which has proved willing to use force in pursuit and defence of its claims. In this context, the recent events in Beijing may bode ill for the future. In China's post-revolutionary history, there seems to be a close correlation between domestic turmoils on the one hand and hardline foreign policy postures on the other. If this should prove to be the case, it is not inconceivable that Beijing might engage in less than benign conduct in its relations with the external world and that the South China Sea will provide the kind of low-risk, low-cost arena for the manifestation of this conduct which is required by China's continuing commitment to an open-door economic policy.

However, it should also be pointed out that, although undoubtedly the most crucial, the South China Sea is by no means the only important 'non-traditional' security problem. Other issues of significance which are potential sources or catalysts of international conflict and tension are the resources of the Mekong River, the timber on mainland Southeast Asia, and fisheries and the environment in maritime Southeast Asia. It was a logging dispute after all that helped to precipitate the chain of events leading up to the bloody border war between Thailand and Laos in 1987-88.

If the foregoing trends take place, a number of consequences are likely to follow.

First, where major actors are concerned, if the United States, the Soviet Union and China scale down their strategic commitments in Southeast Asia, as anticipated above, and if there are no qualitative, as opposed to incremental, changes in Japan's military strength, a balance of political and diplomatic presence is likely to evolve among the four major actors involved in the affairs of the region. This balance, moreover, is likely to be strengthened by the increased presence in Southeast Asia of the European Community, Canada, Australia and New Zealand, which will be attracted by the prospect of prosperity in the region and welcomed by regional states seeking to diversify economic ties.

Second, the growing recognition of the importance of economics, especially in Indochina and Burma, is a trend which is likely to confer disproportionately large benefits upon Japan. To be sure, countries such as Thailand and China, with their geographical advantages, and Australia, with its good relations with Hanoi and Vientiane, are bound to make significant gains from the 'opening up' process taking place in the Indochinese countries and Burma. But it will be Japan, with its immense financial and technological resources, which has the wherewithal to fully assist these countries in accelerating their economic development and hence to reap gains therefrom. The end of the century is likely to see a fully fledged, region-wide economic *Pax Japonica* in Southeast Asia.

Third, the reduction of great power competition both at the global and at the regional level, the growing recognition of the importance of economics, and the domestic trends taking place in Indochina and Thailand, are likely to lead to a decline of Vietnamese-Thai rivalry for the 'trans-Mekong region'. This region, comprising the lowland parts of contemporary Laos and most of contemporary Cambodia has, since the early 18th century, been the object of competition, armed or otherwise, between the centre of power in the Chao Phraya River plains on the one hand and that in the Red River Delta on the other. The region in question has no easily defensible natural barrier that could keep the centres of power separated and satisfied with their separation. In one sense the present conflict over Cambodia is but the latest chapter of this historic competition.

Geostrategic factors and a legacy of long-held mutual distrust mean that this rivalry is unlikely to disappear altogether. But domestic economic imperatives in the context of reduced global and regional tension will in all probability make the two rivals economic partners — somewhat uneasy and less-than-full partners to be sure, but partners nevertheless. Thailand's demand for and Vietnam's ability to supply raw materials may be important in the early stages of this evolving partnership. But in the longer term the more crucial factor will be Thailand's ability to act as both a provider of and a conduit for investment, technology and services much needed by Vietnam, for example in agro-industry, telecommunications, tourism, banking and insurance. Significantly, in a meeting of Southeast Asian central bankers in Bangkok in January 1989, Hanoi's representatives, together with their counterparts from Laos, approached the Thais to explore the possibility of their using the Thai baht as their reserve currency.

This economic partnership between Vietnam and Thailand is developing and is likely to evolve further even though there is no comprehensive settlement of the Cambodian conflict or a likelihood of one.

Vietnam may be willing to withdraw its troops to decrease its military burden, to satisfy its Soviet ally and to gain access to the economic resources of the non-communist world. But there is no indication that it is or will be prepared to abandon all political influence over Cambodia and Laos. Evidence suggests that Hanoi still sees Indochina as a single strategic unit, primacy over which is a *sine qua non* of its security. It is highly significant that the April 5, 1989 declaration of Vietnam's unilateral military withdrawal by the end of September 1989 was not a unilateral statement but one made by all three Indochinese countries and that the possibility of Vietnam's return in the event of deterioration of the internal situation in Cambodia was more or less clearly spelled out for the first time. According to most sources of information, the Khmer Rouge still possesses large quantities of arms, extensive political networks within Cambodia and a sizeable hard core of experienced and committed fighters. As long as this remains the case, there is little likelihood of a comprehensive settlement. The possibility of a more extensive civil war and hence the return of Vietnamese troops to Cambodia thus cannot be ruled out.

For its part, Thailand is unlikely to be willing to endorse an arrangement in Cambodia which institutionalises Vietnamese primacy or one which clearly embodies a denial of China's right to participate in the determination of the course of regional affairs. In absence of a comprehensive settlement the Thais are likely to 'hedge their bets' and continue the policy of providing support to the armed resistance movements, particularly the Khmer Rouge, although most certainly at a lower level than before, given the general improvement in Thai-Vietnamese relations. This continuing support will in turn make a comprehensive solution even more elusive.

But at the same time, as long as Vietnamese troops remain out of Cambodia, and ways and means of keeping most of the Vietnamese troops out of Cambodia can be found, Bangkok will be more or less satisfied that there is no clear and present danger to itself. Accordingly it will not be reluctant to conduct 'business-as-usual' relations with Hanoi, especially if one considers the fact that the prospects for reaping benefits from improved economic ties with Vietnam are generally thought to be good. Moreover Thailand is likely to be further attracted by the prospect of improved ties with Laos and a Vietnamese-influenced regime in Phnom Penh — attracted not only by the raw materials and investment opportunities available but also by the hope that one day history may be 'reversed' and that closer ties with Thailand would 'wean' the two away from Vietnam.

The trend towards peaceful coexistence and 'business-as-usual' relations between Vietnam and Thailand is one which will make it more difficult to achieve a comprehensive solution to the Cambodian problem. Thus the prospect of its taking place is looked upon as being undesirable by those who advocate a 'just and durable' settlement, whereby Cambodia becomes completely free of Vietnamese influence and fully democratic. Indeed, the possibility that those who reject such a *de facto* acceptance of Vietnam's position in Cambodia may create problems which would increase tension once more cannot be rulled out. But there is little doubt that, at least in the short term, this trend has contributed and will continue to contribute to the process of rapprochement and detente in international politics at the global and regional levels, and that at this juncture with China preoccupied with domestic problems, there is no party, except the Khmer Rouge, which has both the willingness and the capacity to reverse such a trend against the wishes of both Vietnam and Thailand.

Fourth, if the present trends continue and if over the longer term Thailand can fully play its role as the provider of and conduit for investment, technology and services — not only for Vietnam and the other two Indochinese countries but also for Burma — there are likely to be increasingly close economic ties among the countries of mainland Southeast Asia. Should this be the case, there is likely to be a 'natural' process whereby Southeast Asia becomes divided into two loose, politically uninstitutionalised economic configurations, one on mainland Southeast Asia with Bangkok as its 'hub', the other in maritime Southeast Asia with Singapore as its 'hub'.

On the basis of the foregoing discussion of major trends related directly or indirectly to the future of Southeast Asia, one can now put forward some proposals regarding the framework for peace and security in the region over the next decade. However, two caveats should be borne in mind. First, these proposals are formulated from the perspective of the regional states, more specifically, the Asean countries. Second, they are not intended to form a blueprint for the future of Southeast Asia but to act as catalysts for further thought and discussion.

Some proposals

First, even though all the trends seem to point towards continued rapprochement and detente among the main actors involved in regional affairs, the likely absence of a comprehensive settlement in Cambodia means that peace will ultimately be fragile. The Khmer Rouge remains the main uncertainty and also the main potential source of destabilisation. After Vietnam's withdrawal, should the Khmer Rouge continue to fight, as most people expect they would, and should they pose sufficient threat to Cambodia's stability, as some people believe they might, a return of the Vietnamese forces cannot be ruled out. Thus the present favourable portents should not be taken as a reason not to strive more urgently for a comprehensive solution to the Cambodian conflict but should be considered a valuable opportunity for working out such a solution.

In this context the first priority for the Asean countries is to find a new consensus regarding the ways and means of resolving the Cambodian conflict — a consensus which is not an uneasy compromise between Thailand and Indonesia, but one which reflects both Indonesia's past favourable dispositions towards Vietnam and Thailand's newly-found flexibility *vis-a-vis* Hanoi. Moreover, the process of forging this new consensus must also take into consideration the Asean countries' growing stature in the councils among nations and the likelihood that, because of the recent turmoil in China, one could not hope for a constructive foreign policy from Beijing for a period of time. Once this new consensus is reached, Asean should proceed to implement it, even if it means that the Asean countries seek a solution without China's full participation or approbation.

While it is acknowledged that the new consensus can only emerge after earnest discussions among the Asean partners and after all perspectives and options have been carefully examined, it might perhaps be useful to make certain more or less concrete suggestions at this juncture. One is that the new consensus should before anything else aim at finding ways and means of avoiding a civil war in the aftermath of Vietnam's withdrawal, or at the very least, containing one, should it prove to be impossible to avert. This is necessary to prevent Vietnam from returning in force, thus reviving once more the Cambodian conflict. If such ways and means require that Thailand change its policy towards the Khmer Rouge in defiance of China, then the Asean partners should lend Bangkok all their support.

Second, the new consensus should aim at providing as fair a deal for the Cambodians as possible and at allowing normalcy to return to their troubled land, for it would serve as the longer-term underpinning of peace in Cambodia. This in turn requires that the Asean countries initiate, or help to initiate, a comprehensive international assistance programme that would make possible repatriation of displaced persons and the long-term development of Cambodia's infrastructure and human resources. It also requires that the Asean countries begin to deal with the situation as it is, rather than continue to engage in wishful thinking about what might have been or will be. To put it bluntly, Asean must begin to deal with the Hun Sen regime which, for better or for worse, is the only Cambodian faction with an effective administrative machinery at its disposal. At the same time it must be impressed upon the Hun Sen group that it must allow the broadening of the base of its regime, with representatives from other Cambodian factions being given opportunities to participate meaningfully in the structure and processes of governance; that such a broadening of the regime's base is necessary for peace and security of the region; and that diplomatic relations can be considered only after this has been achieved.

A new Asean consensus over Cambodia is necessary because there are a number of issue areas where the six members need to cooperate in order to strengthen the fabric of peace and security in the region.

One such issue area is great power presence in Southeast Asia. The Asean countries since 1971 have advocated that the region be transformed into a Zone of Peace, Freedom and Neutrality, and until now ZOPFAN has seemed to be no more than an empty aspiration or rhetoric. At present, with the trends towards a decline of the great powers' military presence and towards a balance of political and diplomatic presence among the major actors, there is an opportunity for translating the idea into practice, not necessarily overnight, but gradually over the next decade.

Similarly with the idea of making Southeast Asia a nuclear-weapons-free zone: the favourable international and regional environments have opened up opportunities for more concrete and sustained initiatives to implement it. A valuable starting point to work for would be to formulate what may be termed 'a self-denying ordinance', whereby all regional states announce that they would not develop, possess or have deployed in their territories nuclear weapons.

Another issue area is dealing with the so-called 'non-traditional' security problems. Before these become more acute and less amenable to control, the Asean countries should make use of the present favourable international climate to strive for the creation of region-wide fishery and environment management regimes. Moreover, concerted efforts should be made to bring all South China Sea littoral states, including China, to the same negotiating table, so that a comprehensive process of working out maritime boundaries and claims to various islands could be initiated.

In order to strengthen the economic underpinning of regional peace and security, the Asean countries must try to find the political will to accelerate intra-Asean economic co-operation. This is necessary, not only to increase the group's bargaining power in an era of rising economic nationalism and economic bloc-building, but also to ensure that the logic of Thai capitalism does not lead to increasing distance between Bangkok and its Asean partners.

At the same time, care should be taken to ensure that greater Asean economic co-operation should not accentuate political divisiveness in Southeast Asia. After Vietnam's withdrawal from Cambodia, all the three Indochinese countries should be given an opportunity to participate fully in the process of global economic development. Thailand's economic ties with these countries should be seen as one of many means of bridge-building between non-communist and communist Southeast Asia. Other means should include a continuation of Indochina's diplomacy *vis-a-vis* Vietnam, which has served and is likely to continue to serve as a crucial factor in promoting greater Asean-Indochinese understanding.

Regarding the question of the expansion of Thai capitalism into Indochina, it should be pointed out that this will not necessarily lead to Thailand's abandonment of Asean, for the expansion is and is likely to remain purely economic and largely fuelled by economic motivations. It should also be pointed out that the real value of Asean lies in its ability to be and remain a relevant and constructive organisation. This is in turn means that it must be more than a club of like-minded political leaders and bureaucrats, far removed from the realities of life, and that it must be able to accommodate and make use of the dynamic changes in the real world. Since one of the most evident dynamic changes today is Thailand's economic growth and expansion, the Asean countries must collectively come to terms with it and gain advantages from it.

Furthermore, to help create a region-wide order over the long term after Vietnam's military withdrawal, a more institutionalised relationship between Asean and Hanoi should be considered, perhaps with the latter being offered the option of acceding to Asean's Treaty of Amity and Co-operation as a first step towards this end.

Since the end of World War II, Southeast Asia has been ravaged by wars and conflicts which caused deep divisions within the region. These wars and conflicts have always involved great powers and hence always proved to be beyond the capacity of regional states to manage or control. However, for the first time now the prevailing trends in the international system have given regional states the opportunity of ameliorating or removing the lines of division within the region, of creating a region-wide order reflecting the needs and requirements of regional states themselves, and of ultimately creating one Southeast Asia — albeit one which would not be free of great power involvement. Indeed geography and the direction of the region's economic development would make that impossible. But greater unity among Southeast Asian states would help to ensure that there would be less opportunity or reason for great power military interventions and that great power involvement could be transformed into positive contributions towards the peace and prosperity of the region. Whether regional states could perform this task remains to be seen.

Appendix A: Report of workshop on the Korean conflict*

ANDREW MACK
Head, Peace Research Centre, Australian National University

THE Korean Workshop brought together individuals from both Koreas as well as the other major powers involved in the conflict for two hours of intensive but — perhaps inevitably — inconclusive discussion. In the workshop, as on the Korean peninsula itself, there was no real consensus as to *how* future progress should be achieved.

This did not mean that there was no consensus about the desired outcome of the Korean conflict — namely a united, peaceful and prosperous Korea. Disagreement was about *means* rather than ends — although the preferred solution of the participants from the North for a confederal state clearly represented a higher degree of political integration than did the commonwealth concept currently preferred by the participants from the South.

There was also a considerable degree of consensus that a number of political developments external to the Korean peninsula were likely to enhance the long-term prospects for a solution. The growing contacts between the major socialist states and South Korea and, to a lesser degree, between North Korea and pro-Western states were seen as being likely to facilitate the search for a solution. But it was noted that while South Korean trade with the North's major allies was expanding rapidly, there had been no parallel growth in trade between the Koreas themselves.

---

* The workshop on the Korean conflict for the purpose of recording areas of agreement with regard to confidence building and conflict resolution

The growing detente between the superpowers was also viewed very positively. As tensions between the US and the USSR declined, each would be less likely to view the Korean conflict as an extension of the Cold War and thus less likely to adopt partisan positions towards its solution.

Although there was considerable disagreement about the nature of the military balance between the two Koreas there seemed to be a general consensus that the military confrontation was — in itself — not merely costly and undesirable but also potentially destabilising. The arms race on the peninsula was not, of course, the cause of the conflict but there was little doubt that it exacerbated it.

There was also wide consensus that unification was a process that had to be conducted exclusively by the Koreans themselves — though many participants argued that the resolution of security issues on the peninsula should be on a multilateral basis and involve the key outside powers.

One participant argued that as the economies of both North and South were transformed by the process of industrialisation the two systems would become more compatible and increased system compatibility was a necessary condition of the long-term task of reunification. It is certainly true that as societies become more complex and interdependent it is increasingly difficult to rule them by coercion and repression. Individuals within complex and interdependent industrial societies are today increasingly indispensable and insubstitutable within the economies of those societies.

This gives them structural power within their society which individuals in simpler societies simply do not have. This, I believe, is a major reason why class warfare has been domesticated in the West over the past 100 years and why the Soviet Union of the 1980s is so much less repressive than that of the 1930s.

Perhaps the greatest disagreement between the participants related to the *means* by which reunification should be achieved.

Participants from the North argued that the division of the two countries was the root cause of the conflict and that reunification was therefore a necessary condition for conflict. Proceeding without a clear and mutually agreed reunification plan was like trying to navigate without a map or build a house without a blueprint.

As one participant put it: The North sees reunificaiton as a necessary condition for peace; the South sees peace as a necessary condition of reunification.

From the North's perspective the question of unification is intimately related to the presence of nuclear-armed foreign forces in the South. Foreign forces not only help perpetuate the division which is the barrier to peace, but their presence is antithetical to the goal of national independence which both sides agreed in 1972 should be one of the three principles of national reunification. Withdrawal of US forces should be accompanied by drastic reductions in conventional forces on both sides to an equal ceiling of some 100,000 troops on each side.

Other participants, including those from the South, argued strongly that focussing on the *form* of any final reunification plan was both premature and likely to be counterproductive. It was not that reunification was undesirable; rather it was simply not feasible in the current context of deep distrust. A necessary condition for progress towards unification was for this distrust to be minimised. *Confidence-building* should therefore be the primary goal of discussions between the two sides, since without trust no progress towards the longer term common goal of reunification could be achieved. Small steps would lead to increased confidence which would permit much greater steps.

Participants from the South hoped that a spirit of *glasnost* and *perestroika* would emerge in the North — as it had with such positive consequences in the Soviet Union. They argued that a new and less confrontationalist mood was emerging in the South and that Seoul was not prepared to make unilateral initiatives towards the North without demanding reciprocation.

But some measures still did require reciprocation — including reuniting divided families and cultural and economic exchanges between the two Koreas. Such measures were themselves confidence-building measures (CBMs) designed to create the basic level of trust which was a necessary — but not sufficient — condition of progress.

Increased communication and people-to-people exchanges are not, of course, without risk for either side. Open borders would create possibilities not only for family reunion and increased trade but also subversion.

There was considerable debate about the need for confidence-building measures — what they were, and what form they should take. In Europe confidence-building measures are a variety of measures which have the express goal of reducing the risks of surprise attack and reducing incentives for pre-emptive or first strike wars. These measures include advanced notification of exercises, exchange of observers on exercises, communication measures such as the US/ Soviet Hotline, pull-back of forces from areas of military confrontation so as to create genuine demilitarised zones and so forth.

At Stanford University, James Goodby, former US ambasador to the Stockholm Conference on confidence-building measures for Europe, has been examining the applicability of European CBMs for the Korean peninsula. His conclusion is that many of the European measures would be both applicable and useful for Korea.

Participants from the North argued that their proposal to reduce troop levels to a common ceiling of 100,000 troops was a confidence-building measure in itself — though their three-year timetable was regarded with scepticism by many participants. There is in fact little doubt that troop level reductions on both sides *would* help dispel some distrust, but the European experience in seeking such reductions has not been very encouraging. The North Atlantic Treaty Organisation (NATO) and the Warsaw Pact negotiated for 14 years at the Mutual and Balanced Force Reduction (MBFR) talks in Vienna without *any* agreement. The Stockholm conference on CBMs, by contrast, yielded a successful agreement in 1986 and progress between the US and the Soviet Union on arms reductions has subsequently been greater than at any time since World War II.

Troop level reductions are certainly a worthwhile medium-term goal, but one of the ironies of arms control is that when it is most needed it is most difficult to achieve. Arms control negotiations require a minimum degree of confidence between the parties at the outset if they are to succeed — this is why it may well be necessary to institute some of the most basic CBMs in Korea if the more far-reaching process of force level reductions is to succeed.

CBMs require above all that each side be sensitive to the other's particular security concerns. Pyongyang needs to be sensitive to the concerns which the South has about the offensive orientation of the North's force structure. The South, on the other hand, should consider seriously whether or not the military benefit which derives from holding the huge Team Spirit exercise every year is worth the political cost in terms of undermining the prospects for confidence-building.

In the longer term there is, as both Soviet and American participants reminded the workshop, a great deal to be learned from the current Soviet drive towards creating a non-provocative force posture which is extremely powerful in defence, but with only the most limited capability for offensive action. Such defensive force postures remove all incentives for striking first in crises and for arms races. They enhance crisis stability and reduce the fear, suspicion and hostility which are the inevitable consequence of offensive force postures — postures which can be used for aggression as well as for defence.

Let me conclude by noting that our workshop — as I indicated in the beginning — did not arrive at any detailed consensus. Insofar as it reflected the real situation on the Korean peninsula this was hardly surprising. But on one issue there was no dissension — all participants agreed that however peace was to be pursued it had to be pursued non-violently. As Winston Churchill once said 'Jaw jaw is better than war war'.

Appendix B: Report of workshop on the Cambodian conflict*

MUTHIAH ALAGAPPA
Senior Research Fellow, International Relations Programme, East-West Centre, Hawaii

IN his welcoming remarks, Chairman MR Kasem S Kasemsri stated that all parties to the conflict appear to be interested in arriving at a political settlement and that a momentum has been generated that will hopefully lead to a settlement in the near future. However, a number of key issues remain unresolved and considerable effort and attention would be required in reconciling differing positions. He viewed this workshop as well-timed to make an invaluable contribution to the proposed international conference on Cambodia in August 1989.

The Chairman identified the following six issues as key to a settlement of the conflict:

(a) Complete withdrawal of Vietnamese troops from Cambodia within a fixed timetable under the effective supervision of an appropriate international mechanism.

(b) Cessation of external military assistance to all Cambodian parties.

(c) The setting up of a national authority of reconciliation, and the subsequent democratic elections basing on the legitimacy of the new state of Cambodia.

(d) The international guarantee of Cambodia's independence, neutrality, its own security and those of her neighbours.

(e) The return of refugees and their rehabilitation in the area of their choice,

---

* The workshop on the Cambodian conflict for the purpose of recording areas of agreement with regard to confidence building and conflict resolution

assisted by competent international institutions.

(f) Reconstruction and development of Cambodia — international involvement.

The workshop participants engaged in a lively and frank exchange of views on a number of these issues. The discussion highlighted the intricate linkages between the various components and the need to adopt a comprehensive and holistic approach to the settlement of the Cambodian conflict. A summary of the discussion of the various issues is appended below.

Withdrawal of Vietnamese troops from Cambodia. It was generally acknowleged that this was a fundamental issue and that Vietnam would, as it had pledged, withdraw its troops from Cambodia by the end of September 1989. However, several concerns were raised:

(a) Would the withdrawal be unilateral or in the context of an internationally negotiated comprehensive settlement? Should withdrawal be linked to an internal settlement?

(b) Would the withdrawal be unconditional or conditional, that is, would it be linked to the cessation of external military assistance and prevention of the return to genocidal policies of the past? Would the Vietnamese troops return if these conditions were not met?

(c) Would the withdrawal be complete and total or would elements be left behind? What would be the implications if elements were indeed left behind?

In additional to a rehearsal of official positions and the raising of the many problems associated with this component, the discussion highlighted the following:

(a) Withdrawal without an amicable internal settlement and effective international supervision would most likely lead to a civil war, thus highlighting the linkage between and the importance of internal settlement and effective international supervision.

(b) Importance of a ceasefire among all parties to the conflict.

(c) There is a strong possibility that some Vietnamese elements will remain behind in Cambodia. This raises a number of questions:

- Would they be able to influence the situation in Cambodia? Would this provide the Khmer Rouge with sufficient cause to pursue its ambitions?
- Would they present a threat to Thailand?
- Would they be a bridgehead for the return of Vietnamese troops?

In other words, would their presence be intolerable or, while not totally satisfactory, can it be accepted as not unduly undermining a settlement that is negotiated?

Prevention of civil war. Many participants expressed the view that a civil war may be inevitable in Cambodia and that its prevention or mitigation must be a high priority for the international community. Several measures to this effect were proposed.

(a) An effective international presence to ensure that the settlement agreed to at the international conference is adhered to.
(b) Cessation of external military assistance to all parties. Without external support, the parties will not have the capacity to engage in full-fledged civil war.
(c) A modicum of national reconciliation among the four factions. The People's Republic of Kampuchea (PRK) government must broaden its base to incorporate elements of the other factions especially that of Prince Sihanouk.

Effective international presence. There was near unanimous agreement that effective international presence in Cambodia was vital to ensure the following:

(a) Supervise the implementation of the ceasefire.
(b) Monitor the withdrawal of the Vietnamese troops.
(c) Supervise the cessation of external military assistance.
(d) Supervise the conduct of elections.
(e) Facilitate confidence building among the various factions in a post-settlement phase.
(f) Prevent the return of Vietnamese troops.

In this connection, the view was expressed that international presence must be concerned with creating the appropriate environment for the regeneration of the Cambodian state and to enable the Cambodian people to freely determine their destiny. While this view calls for a substantial or massive international presence, an alternate view calls for minimum presence with emphasis being placed on reconciliation among the Khmer factions and entrusting the law and order function essentially to the Khmers themselves.

There was considerable discussion of the appropriate form of the international mechanism for Cambodia. One view was that the United Nations had been impartial and that, unless at the minimun leave the Cambodian seat in the UN vacant, the UN should not play a role in Cambodia. The favoured mechanism of this viewpoint was an enlarged International Consultative Council. Those who argued for a UN role cited the institutional structure and therefore its capacity, its experience and expertise to undertake this function. It was also pointed out that the UN *is* the international community and also that the major powers were working towards strengthening the UN as an institution for world peace and security. It was also pointed out that the United Nations General Assembly (UNGA) was only one of the UN organs and that the UN Security Council and the UN Secretariat can effectively undertake this responsibility in Cambodia. It was also suggested that the UN peacekeeping force could comprise members from the non-aligned movement acceptable to all parties to the conflict. The need to distinguish between political and military tasks and to entrust them to separate agencies was also pointed out. The acceptability of the UN would also, it was argued, depend on the acceptability of the internal settlement to Vietnam.

Setting up of a national authority of reconciliation. Power sharing among the four factions was acknowledged as a central and critical issue. Several viewpoints were expressed on the issue of power sharing:

(a) Power sharing should not be an international concern and should be left to the four Khmer factions to decide. Formation of a quadripartite government before elections will be a violation of the Kampuchean peoples' rights.

(b) The international community has an obligation to put together a coalition government and to prevent domination by any one faction.

(c) National reconciliation and power sharing is virtually impossible in a political culture that has no such tradition. Each party views the outcome in terms of winning and losing and as the stakes are high, every possible measure and avenue will be used to gain dominance.

(d) Khmer nationalism and the force of circumstances will induce reconciliation and some power sharing.

(e) The Khmer Rouge will not be willing to share power and will strive for dominance.

(f) It is possible to form a coalition of two or three factions minus the Khmer Rouge and this will be a viable coalition.

(g) The Khmer Rouge must form part of any coalition. Otherwise the settlement will not be acceptable to all parties and will break down.

Preventing the return of the Khmer Rouge to exclusive control in Cambodia.
There was unanimous agreement that the Khmer Rouge must be prevented from returning to exclusive control in Cambodia. Measures proposed to achieve this included the following:

(a) Effective international presence and cessation of external military assistance. In this connection, Thailand will have to play a key role in addressing the problem of the Khmer Rouge and Asean should support the Thai position.

(b) An arrangement that incorporates the legitimacy of Prince Sihanouk and the power of the PRK with international support may be able to contain the Khmer Rouge.

Democratic elections. Democratic elections are important but priority should also be accorded to the regeneration of the Cambodian state and to create sufficient and viable options to allow meaningful choice for the Cambodian people.

Conclusion

Time constraint prevented a more detailed exploration of the issues identified by the Chairman. Although no consensus emerged, several participants, pointing to the many positive trends at the global, regional and sub-regional levels and also the changing realities in the countries and parties involved, expressed optimism that a settlement could be worked out. They, however, stressed that under the circumstances what should be aimed for is a 'tolerable' and not an 'ideal' settlement and that the goal must be to provide the Cambodian people with as best a deal as possible. The international community had an obligation and an important role to play in ensuring the regeneration of the Cambodian state and its security.

List of participating individuals*

Mr Abdul Hai Haji Zawawi
Undersecretary, Ministry of Defence, Malaysia

***High Commissioner Pengiran Dipa Negara Laila DiRaja
 Haji Abdul Momin bin Pengiran Haji Ismail***
High Commissioner of Brunei to Malaysia

Datuk Abdul Rahim Mohd Noor
Ministry of Home Affairs, Malaysia

Maj Gen Raja Dato' Abdul Rashid Raja Badiozaman
Chief of Intelligence Staff, Ministry of Defence, Malaysia

Mr Ahmad Khalid
Prime Minister's Department, Malaysia

Mr Ahn Ho Young
Institute for Foreign Affairs and National Security, Ministry of Foreign Affairs,
Republic of Korea

Mr Y V Akhrimenko
Executive Secretary, Soviet National Committee on Asia-Pacific Economic
Cooperation, USSR

Dr Muthiah Alagappa
Senior Research Fellow, International Relations Programme, East-West Centre,
Hawaii

Mr David Arase
Assistant Professor, Department of Government, Pomona College, California,
United States

Dato' Raja Ariffin Raja Sulaiman
Deputy Minister, Prime Minister's Department, Malaysia

Mr E P Bazhanov
International Department, Central Committee CPSU, USSR

Mr Jacques Bekaert
Special Correspondent, *The Bangkok Post*, Thailand

Dr James A Boutilier
Dean, Faculty of Arts, Royal Roads Military College, Victoria,
British Columbia, Canada

---

* Designations and affiliations as at June 1989

Professor Kend Calder
Woodrow Wilson School of Public and International Affairs,
Princeton University, New Jersey, United States

Mr Chen Zhiya
Research Fellow, Institute of International Strategic Studies of China,
Centre for International Studies, Beijing, China

Dr Gennady I Chufrin
Head of Department, Institute of Oriental Studies, Academy of Science, USSR

Dr In-Young Chun
College of Education, Seoul National University, Republic of Korea

Mr Chung Mong-Joon
Chairman, Hyundai Heavy Industries, Republic of Korea

Ms Clara Joewono
Director of Public Affairs, Centre for Strategic and International Studies,
Indonesia

Mr Tran Quang Co
Deputy Minister of Foreign Affairs, Vietnam

Mr Christopher C Coleman
Director of Dispute Settlement and Negotiation Programmes, International
Peace Academy, United Nations

Professor Gerald Curtis
Director, East Asian Institute, Columbia University, New York, United States

Congressman Jose de Venecia
Chairman, House Committee on Foreign Relations, the Philippines

Mr Doungdy Khanthavilay
Ministry of Foreign Affairs, Laos

Mr Nick Etheridge
Director, Political and Strategic Analysis Division, Department of External
Affairs, Ottawa, Canada

Professor Peggy Falkenheim
Department of Political Science, University of Western Ontario, London,
Canada

Mr Trevor Findlay
Senior Research Fellow, Peace Research Centre, Research School of Pacific
Studies, Australian National University, Canberra, Australia

Mr Gao E
Deputy Director-General, Centre for International Studies, Beijing, China

Mr Jeffrey B Gayner
Counsellor for International Affairs, Heritage Foundation, United States

Mr Francois Gipouloux
Research Fellow, National Centre of Scientific Research, France

Mr Andrei E Granovsky
Counsellor, Arms Control Directorate, Ministry of Foreign Affairs, USSR

Ambassador Hasnan Habib
Centre for Strategic and International Studies, Indonesia

Mr Warwick Hawker
Deputy High Commissioner of New Zealand to Malaysia

High Commissioner Cavan Hogue
High Commissioner of Australia to Malaysia

Mr Thomas C Hubbard
Chargé d'Affaires, Embassy of the United States of America, Kuala Lumpur, Malaysia

Ambassador Cao Duc Hung
Ambassador of Vietnam to Malaysia

Tun Hussein Onn
Former Prime Minister of Malaysia and Chairman, ISIS Malaysia

Mr Kadir Jasin
Group Editor, *The New Straits Times*, Malaysia

M R Kasem S Kasemsri
Permanent Secretary, Ministry of Foreign Affairs, Thailand

Mr Harry Kendall
Institute of East Asian Studies, University of California, Berkeley, United States

Mr Anthony C Kevin
Assistant Secretary, Policy Planning Branch, Department of Foreign Affairs and Trade, Canberra, Australia

Mr Khairuddin Ibrahim
Secretary, National Security Council, Prime Minister's Department, Malaysia

Col B V Khilko
Deputy Head of Department, Ministry of Defence, USSR

Mr Uch Kiman
Ministry of Foreign Affairs, Phnom Penh, Cambodia

Mr M S Koliada
Counsellor, Embassy of the Union of Soviet Socialist Republics, Malaysia

Dr Kusuma Snitwongse
Faculty of Political Science, Chulalongkorn University, Thailand

Dr Lao Mong Hay
Representative of the Khmer People's National Liberation Front (KPNLF)

Dr Lau Teik Soon
Department of Political Science, National University of Singapore, Singapore

Dr Lee Young Ho
President, Korea Policy Research Centre, Republic of Korea

Dr Michael Leifer
Department of International Relations, London School of Economics and Political Science, Britain

Dr Norman D Levin
The Rand Corporation, California, United States

Dr Hank Lim
Senior Lecturer, Department of Economics and Statistics, National University of Singapore, Singapore

Mr Jose Apolinario Lozada Jr
Head, Legislative Staff, Senate Committee on Foreign Relations, the Philippines

Dr V P Lukin
Deputy Head of Department, Ministry of Foreign Affairs, USSR

Mr Andrew Mack
Head, Peace Research Centre, Research School of Pacific Studies, Australian National University, Canberra, Australia

Mr Kishore Mahbubani
Deputy Secretary, Ministry of Foreign Affairs, Singapore

Datuk Majid Mohamed
Deputy Secretary-General I, Ministry of Foreign Affairs, Malaysia

Mr Hiroshi Matsumoto
Association for Promotion of International Cooperation, Japan

**Pehin Orang Kaya Seri Dewa Dato Seri Pahlawan
  Haji Mohammad bin Haji Daud**
Chief of Armed Forces, Negara Brunei Darussalam

Dato Paduka Awang Haji Mohamad Alimin bin Haji Abdul Wahab
Permanent Secretary, Ministry of Defence, Negara Brunei Darussalam

Ambassador Mohamed Haron
Deputy Secretary-General II, Ministry of Foreign Affairs, Malaysia

Tan Sri Mohd Haniff bin Omar
Inspector-General of Police, Royal Malaysian Police, Malaysia

Prof Noel V Morada
Department of Political Science, University of the Philippines

Ambassador Noburu Nakahira
Ambassador of Japan to Malaysia

Mr Osamu Nariai
International Institute for Global Peace, Japan

High Commissioner Dr S R Nathan
High Commissioner of Singapore to Malaysia

Mr Bui Xuan Ninh
Senior Research Fellow, Institute for International Relations, Ministry of
Foreign Affairs, Vietnam

Mr Wataru Nishigahiro
Counsellor for Political Affairs, Embassy of Japan, Kuala Lumpur, Malaysia

Mr Yoshiji Nogami
Executive Director, Japan Institute for International Affairs, Japan

Datuk Haji Noordin Omar
Ministry of Home Affairs, Malaysia

Dr Noordin Sopiee
Director-General, ISIS Malaysia

Professor T John Pempel
Department of Government, Cornell University, Ithaca, New York,
United States

Mr Keo Rasmey
Head, Department of Foreign Affairs, Office of the Personal Representative of
Prince Norodom Sihanouk in Kampuchea and Asia

Professor Rhee Sang-Woo
Dean, Graduate School of Public Policy, Sogang University, Republic of Korea

Mr Michael Richardson
Editor for Asia, *International Herald Tribune,* Singapore

Ms Rohana Mahmood
Analyst, ISIS Malaysia

Ambassador Rongpet Sucharitkul
Ambassador of Thailand to Malaysia

Tan Sri Rozhan Kuntom
Distinguished Fellow, ISIS Malaysia and Chairman, Cooperative Central Bank, Malaysia

Mr Rye Sung Chol
Deputy Chairman, Institute for Disarmament and Peace, Democratic People's Republic of Korea

Mr Sabam Siagian
Chief Editor, *The Jakarta Post*, Indonesia

Professor K S Sandhu
Director, Institute of Southeast Asian Studies, Singapore

Professor Robert A Scalapino
Director, Institute of East Asian Studies, University of California, Berkeley, United States

Ambassador Rodolfo Severino Jr
Ambassador of the Philippines to Malaysia

Senator Leticia Ramos Shahani
Chairman, Senate Committee on Foreign Relations, the Philippines

Mr Glenn R Sheppy
Counsellor, Canadian High Commission, Kuala Lumpur, Malaysia

Maj Gen (Rtd) Hiroshi Shimizu
Research Institute for Peace and Security, Japan

Dr Takahashi Shirasu
Chief Programme Officer, Sasakawa Peace Foundation, Japan

Dr Soedjati Djiwandono
Centre for Strategic and International Studies, Indonesia

Mr Soendaroe Rachmad
Head, Centre for Foreign Political Affairs, Department of Foreign Affairs, Indonesia

Mdm Sofiah Taha
Research Officer, Ministry of Defence, Negara Brunei Darussalam

Ambassador Dr Sohn Jang Nai
Ambassador of the Republic of Korea to Malaysia

Mr Max Soliven
Publisher and Editor-in-Chief, *The Philippine Star*, the Philippines

Mr Soubanh Srithirath
Vice Minister of Foreign Affairs, Laos

High Commissioner JNT Spreckley
High Commissioner of Britain to Malaysia

Dr Elpidio Sta Romana
Department of Political Science, University of the Philippines

Professor Richard Stubbs
Associate Director, Joint Centre for Asia Pacific Studies, Department of
Political Science, University of Toronto, Canada

M R Sukhumbhand Paribatra
Director, Institute of Security and International Studies, Chulalongkorn
University, Thailand

Ambassador Sunarso Djajusman
Ambassador of the Republic of Indonesia to Malaysia

Dr Kazuo Takahashi
Programme Director, Sasakawa Peace Foundation, Japan

Mr Nobuyuki Takaki
Editorial Writer, *Mainichi Shimbun*, Japan

Mr Yasuhiro Takeda
International Institute for Global Peace, Japan

Ms Sandra Tarte
Lecturer in Politics, Department of History and Politics, University of the South
Pacific, Suva, Fiji

Dr Ramesh Thakur
Senior Lecturer, Department of Political Studies, Otago University,
New Zealand

Mr Katsuichi Tsukamoto
Executive Director, Research Institute for Peace and Security, Japan

Ambassador U Ba Nyunt
Ambassador of the Socialist Republic of the Union of Burma to Malaysia

Ms Khatharya Um
Department of Political Science, University of California, Berkeley,
United States

Mr Thierry Vankerk-Hoven
Counsellor, Embassy of the Republic of France, Kuala Lumpur, Malaysia

Gen Tan Sri Dato' Yaacob Mohd Zain
Chief of Army, Ministry of Defence, Malaysia

Ambassador Yahya Baba
Director-General of Southeast Asia/Australia/New Zealand/Pacific,
Ministry of Foreign Affairs, Malaysia

Mr Yang Jiemian
Research Fellow and Director of Academic Affairs, Shanghai Institute of
International Studies, China

Dr Emmanuel Yap
Senior Advisor, Senate Committee on Foreign Relations, the Philippines

Mr Ye Lin
Advisor and Research Fellow, Centre for International Studies, Beijing, China

Mr Ye Yong Song
Researcher, Institute for Disarmament and Peace, Democratic People's Republic
of Korea

Ambassador Yu Jae Han
Ambassador of the Democratic People's Republic of Korea to Malaysia

Mr Yun Gyong Chou
Second Secretary, Embassy of the Democratic People's Republic of Korea,
Kuala Lumpur, Malaysia

Professor Donald Zagoria
Hunter College and Harriman, Columbia University, New York, United States

Tan Sri Zainal Abidin Sulong
Distinguished Fellow, ISIS Malaysia and Chairman, Malaysian Industrial
Development Authority

Tan Sri Zakaria Mohd Ali
Distinguished Fellow, ISIS Malaysia and Chairman, UMW, Malaysia

Ambassador Zhou Gang
Ambassador of the People's Republic of China to Malaysia

Mr Zhu Suhua
Associate Research Fellow, Research Centre of the Chinese Association for
International Understanding, Centre for International Studies, Beijing, China

Mr Zulkifli Abdullah
Head, Centre for International Relations and Strategic Studies, National Institute
of Public Administration, Malaysia

Observers

Lt Gen (Rtd) Dato' Haji Abdul Jamil Haji Ahmad
Board Member, ISIS Malaysia and Deputy Executive Chairman,
Kontena Nasional Sdn Bhd, Malaysia

Datuk Abdul Khalid Ibrahim
Board Member, ISIS Malaysia and Chief Executive/General Manager,
Permodalan Nasional Berhad, Malaysia

Ungku Adnan Ismail
National Security Council, Prime Minister's Department, Malaysia

Mr Andy J Andrews
Representative, The Asia Foundation, Malaysia

Mrs Paddy Bowie
Paddy Schubert Sdn Bhd, Malaysia

Dr Leszek Buszynski
Senior Research Fellow, Strategic and Defence Studies Centre, Research School
of Pacific Studies, Australian National University, Australia

Col Chung Hyung Jin
Defence and Armed Forces Attache, Embassy of the Republic of Korea,
Kuala Lumpur, Malaysia

Mr Hideo Date
First Secretary, Embassy of Japan, Kuala Lumpur, Malaysia

Mr Wisnu Dewanto
Assistant for Asean activities, Centre for Strategic and International Studies,
Indonesia

Mr Nguyen Thac Dinh
Third Secretary, Embassy of the People's Republic of Vietnam, Kuala Lumpur,
Malaysia

Dr H J Esderts
Project Manager, Freiderich Ebert Stiftung, Malaysia

Mrs Denise Fisher
Australian High Commission, Kuala Lumpur, Malaysia

Mr Patrick Freeman
Political Officer, Embassy of the United States of America, Kuala Lumpur,
Malaysia

Ms Hamidah Yusoff
Special Assistant to the Prime Minister of Malaysia

Mr John Heffern
Political Officer, Embassy of the United States of America, Kuala Lumpur, Malaysia

Mr Clifford F Herbert
Secretary, Economic and International Division, Ministry of Finance, Malaysia

Mr Idris Junid
Prime Minister's Department, Malaysia

Mr Rob Ironmonger
Canada-Asean Centre, Singapore

Mr James Kidner
Second Secretary, British High Commission, Kuala Lumpur, Malaysia

Mr Thomas Lawo
Konrad Adenauer Stiftung, Malaysia

Dr Lee Poh Ping
Associate Professor, Faculty of Economics and Administration, University of Malaya, Malaysia

Ms P G Lim
Board Member, ISIS Malaysia and Director, Regional Centre for Arbitration, Malaysia

Mr Varghese Mathews
First Secretary, High Commission of the Republic of Singapore, Kuala Lumpur, Malaysia

Mr Hal Meinheit
Political Counsellor, Embassy of the United States of America, Kuala Lumpur, Malaysia

Mr Jim Melanson
Deputy Director (Planning and Operations), Development Cooperation Programme, Canada-Asean Centre, Singapore

Mr Denny Mills
First Secretary (Legal), Australian High Commission, Singapore

Dato' Mohamed Sopiee
Board Member, ISIS Malaysia

Dr Munir Majid
Executive Director, Commerce International Merchant Bankers, Malaysia

Dr K S Nathan
Department of History, University of Malaya, Malaysia

Ms Nazirah Hussein
Principal Assistant Secretary, Planning and Research, Ministry of Foreign Affairs, Malaysia

Tun Dato' Omar Yoke Lin Ong
Board Member, ISIS Malaysia

Mr Ong Keng Yong
Counsellor, High Commission of the Republic of Singapore, Kuala Lumpur, Malaysia

Mr Paik Nak Whan
Minister, Embassy of the Republic of Korea, Kuala Lumpur, Malaysia

Mr M Pathmanathan
Faculty of Economics and Administration, University of Malaya, Malaysia

Mr James Pollock
Director, United States Information Service, Embassy of the United States of America, Kuala Lumpur, Malaysia

Mr Razak Baginda
Head, Strategic Studies and International Relations, Ministry of Defence, Malaysia

Mr Peter Redshaw
Counsellor, British High Commission, Kuala Lumpur, Malaysia

Dr Wolfgang Sachsenroeder
Freiderich Naumann Stiftung, Singapore

Mr Charivat Santaputra
First Secretary, Royal Thai Embassy, Kuala Lumpur, Malaysia

Mr Francois Sastourne
First Secretary, Embassy of the Republic of France, Malaysia

Senator Tan Sri C Selvarajah
Board Member, ISIS Malaysia and Deputy Chairman, UMW, Malaysia

Ms Siti Azizah Abod
Principal Assistant Secretary, Ministry of Defence, Malaysia

Tan Sri Dr Tan Chee Khoon
Board Member, ISIS Malaysia

Mr Tham Siew Kuan
Royal Malaysian Police, Malaysia

Mr Alexander Thompson
British Broadcasting Corporation

Mr Mark J Valencia
Visiting Fellow, ISIS Malaysia

Mr Wan A Hamid
Board Member, ISIS Malaysia

Professor Datuk Zainal Abidin Abdul Wahid
Department of History, Universiti Kebangsaan Malaysia, Malaysia

Mr Zainal Abidin Jamaluddin
Prime Minister's Department, Malaysia

Mdm Zakiah Awang
Prime Minister's Department, Malaysia

Dr Zainal Aznam Yusof
Deputy Executive Director, Malaysian Institute for Economic Research, Malaysia

Mr Zhang Bin-Hua
First Secretary, Embassy of the People's Republic of China, Kuala Lumpur, Malaysia